Creating Psychological Safety

TONY HUMPHREYS

Creating Psychological Safety

First published in 2020 by

Panoma Press Ltd
48 St Vincent Drive, St Albans, Herts, AL1 5SJ, UK
info@panomapress.com
www.panomapress.com

Book layout by Neil Coe.

978-1-784529-18-5

The right of Tony Humphreys to be identified as the author of this work has been asserted in accordance with sections 77 and 78 of the Copyright, Designs and Patents Act 1988.

A CIP catalogue record for this book is available from the British Library.

All rights reserved. No part of this book may be reproduced in any material form (including photocopying or storing in any medium by electronic means and whether or not transiently or incidentally to some other use of this publication) without the written permission of the copyright holder except in accordance with the provisions of the Copyright, Designs and Patents Act 1988. Applications for the copyright holder's written permission to reproduce any part of this publication should be addressed to the publishers.

This book is available online and in bookstores.

Copyright 2020 Tony Humphreys

Testimonial by Ann McGarry

Tony Humphreys' *Creating Psychological Safety* presents a groundbreaking departure from the general approaches taken to date on this subject.

Tony Humphreys masterfully introduces the primary theme placing us at centre stage by describing psychological safety as an inside-outside job.

The ultimate psychological safety environment he describes as inhabiting 'I-land', consciously creating boundaries as opposed to protectors that uphold your presence, your own values and beliefs in the face of any unconscious attempts by others to invade your I-land. The relationship that needs most attending is the relationship with Self; and living your own individual life. By doing so, you model, support and create the psychological safety opportunities for others to consciously inhabit their own individuality and live their own unique lives – step by step. When you truly are conscious of your own genius, you will never doubt for one second the other's genius.

Through the carefully scripted, thought provoking narrative, weaved with stories from his own life and client's examples, we learn of personal effectiveness, consciously living from the inside out to experience awe of our own unique presence and that of others. The conscious heroic journey of finding psychological safety is facilitated through the wisdom, spirituality and mastery outlined in the book.

I highly recommend *Creating Psychological Safety* as a must read for parents, teachers, leaders and managers.

Ann McGarry
Human Development Consultant & Author of *CARE of Leadership: A practice for developing leadership effectiveness*

Testimonial by Margaret McCarthy

I would love that all parents, teachers leaders and managers would want to read this book as it provides a very profound and deep understanding of the meaning of Psychological Safety and how Psychological Safety is absolutely crucial to the wellbeing of adults, children and wider society.

When reading through a draft copy of this book, because of the Psychological Safety which I experience in my relationship with Tony, I was free to express difference and explore possibilities with Tony. Psychological Safety in action!

The journey to Personal Conscious Psychological Safety has been and continues to be a long, exciting, at times painful, adventurous journey inwards involving the examination of my story, getting under my pain and suffering, having compassionate understanding of my unconscious psychological safeguards geniusly created by me for my survival. Tony continues to accompany me on this journey creating the psychological safety holding necessary for me to examine my own life and develop a consciousness of my own unique presence and unconditional lovability and capability. Tony accompanies me and others from their own inner personal conscious psychological safety developed through Continuous Personal Reflection, the continuing examination of their lives and the deepening of relationship with themselves. This is the central core message in this book.

We know from research that organisations whose leaders bring their psychological safety/fearlessness to their relationships experienced higher levels of work performance, lower mortality, and embraced conflict as an opportunity for sharing ideas and differences. This book in my opinion goes much deeper in really explaining how it is that the fearless parent, teacher, leader, manager comes to be in such a psychological safety place. Parents, teachers, leaders and managers need to awaken to their unconscious, fear-driven responses as conscious psychological safety leaders are the key players in determining the nature of relationships in the home, school, community and workplace.

To my mentor and colleague Tony I thank you for this book and for all the books; for the consistent and persistent love, support and understanding shown to me at every turn; for enabling me to set myself free and find such peace, love and belief in myself.

With much love and gratitude

Margaret McCarthy
Co-creational Psychotherapist and Chartered Psychologist Ps.SI

Contents

Introduction   6

Chapter One: Radiant Mind   15

Chapter Two: Radiant Start   25

Chapter Three: Psychological Safeguarding   47

Chapter Four: Psychological Safety in Homes and Schools   65

Chapter Five: Parents' Psychological Safety First   81

Chapter Six: Teachers' Psychological Safety First   91

Chapter Seven: Psychological Safety vs Safeguarding Schools   107

Chapter Eight: The Difference Between Safety and Safeguarding   127

Chapter Nine: Psychological Safety Teaching,
              Leadership and Management   145

Chapter Ten: Psychological Safety
           Workplace Relationships   161

Chapter Eleven: Beyond Psychological Safety   171

References   177

Books Tony Humphreys and Helen Ruddle   180

Books Tony Humphreys   180

CDs Tony Humphreys   181

About the Author   182

Index   183

Introduction

The mounting evidence that there is a genius in all of us (Shenk, 2010) means that ingenuity cannot but be present all of the time. Shenk suggests genius needs to be nurtured but this runs counter to his finding that genius is in all of us. How do you nurture what is already there? What does make sense is that *all* behaviour is ingenious – no matter its nature – and our response to it has to be also ingenious. Freud wrote about the distressing contrast between the radiant intelligence of the child and the feeble mentality of the average adult. Somehow Freud missed that what he calls "feeble mentality" is also radiant, also ingenious – but then that is where Freud was at and where you are at is where you need to be! Equally, my response to both Shenk and Freud is where I am at. The difference between us is the level of consciousness that is present within each of us.

There is no suggestion here that Shenk's and Freud's observations are less ingenious than mine; on the contrary, where each of us is, is always ingenious. Neither is there any suggestion that consciousness is more ingenious than unconsciousness. The question here is if the 'average adult' about whom Freud writes is no less ingenious than the 'radiant child', how is it that the child's expression of genius is radically different from most adults? Furthermore, every 'average adult' was once a child and presumably manifested the radiant mind of which Freud was clearly in awe. So, what changed for them that their expression of their genius switched from radiance to feebleness?

What may have triggered the change was the level of *psychological safety* so that threats that emerged in their holding worlds of home, school and community – physical, emotional, sexual, behavioural, intellectual, social and creative – led them to switch their ingenuity from living to surviving. If you give any hint that you are being critical of where another is at or are verbally prescriptive in what they should best do, then you pose a threat to their wellbeing and, if you do, they will very cleverly find a way to appease, attack, knock or ignore or dismiss what you are saying. But if you express your difference as being about where you are, and show a genuine interest in their responses, then an interesting discussion is likely to emerge and you may learn something from each other or amicably agree to differ. Conscious genius now stays open and has no need to resort to psychological safeguarding manoeuvres.

In examining the nature of human genius, the focus needs to be on the psychosocial-physical-sexual contexts of the individual's life and the nature of these contexts − whether threatening or encouraging and supportive − will determine how genius will manifest itself − radiantly or feebly. Also pertinent is how the leaders of particular holding worlds express their genius − in unconscious genius or conscious genius ways. Unconscious genius refers to the situation where individuals in the face of threats create multiple safeguarding/protective screens or walls to ward off and reduce the impact of the threats they are daily encountering. When children encounter the unconscious genius psychological safeguards of the significant adults in their lives, they, like their carers and educators, will counter with their unconscious psychological safeguarding behaviours. Unless these children and their adult mentors find psychological safety (where little or no threat is present) each will maintain their ingeniously creative protective walls.

Be assured that every person wants to express their genius in a conscious genius and uninhibited way and they possess an inner knowing that detects when psychological safety is present. Naturally and wisely they will initially test the waters − 'put their toe in'. When the safe psychological holding is steadfastly maintained, what emerges is conscious genius ways of thriving as opposed to what had been vital for their survival − unconscious genius ways.

How then can the whole topic of human genius be explored without being critical or threatening in any way? What strikes me is that when psychological safety is present, conscious resonance arises – that ingenious internal authority or knowing that knows what is true for one. Equally, when physical and/or psychosocial threats are present, unconscious resonance may arise and may immediately and wisely move to create safeguards/protectors. I say 'may' because when a person at the receiving end of the protective (unconscious) responses of another manages to stay in a conscious psychological safety place, he will maintain a boundary around his own person and not personalise the other's behaviour.

Given the foregoing, the author is then faced with the task of writing this book in a way that the reader will experience profound psychological safety and possibly a shift from unconscious to conscious genius, while experiencing and appreciating the ingenuity of both manifestations. Certainly, I would like to show what psychological safety means in the different holding worlds we inhabit – home, school, community, church, workplace, health, social care environment and sport and leisure environments. Of course, psychological safety is only possible when individuals – most especially those who hold positions of power – are operating from a conscious psychological safety place. Identifying the myriad of ways in which the latter manifests itself may also mirror for the reader where he or she is presently. This mirroring of the characteristics of conscious psychological safety in the presence of the author's safe psychological holding may bring to light what is present and also what has needed to be hidden.

In the same way, in mirroring for the reader the multiple ways in which being conscious genius reveals itself may trigger that conscious resonance – that 'ah ha' moment – for the reader. When the latter occurs a gradual re-emergence of conscious genius happens. Ongoing psychological safety is the sine qua non for that wonderful process to continue.

Clearly, when genius is expressed in conscious genius ways everybody gains. The psychological safety required for the latter to emerge is where consciousness of each person's amazing nature is actively present and, indeed, jealously nurtured. The contrary operates when genius is largely expressed in unconscious ways. Many of the psychological safeguards secretly created in the face of threats in turn become threats to the wellbeing of others – for example: aggression, depression, passivity, violence, harsh criticism, absence of love, presence of conditional relating, perfectionism, addictions.

Other safeguarding responses – what I call protective ways of getting attention in the face of non-attention to one's presence and awesome nature – may also pose threats to the wellbeing of others. Examples are gaining protective recognition through work, success, sports achievement, musical prowess, fame as a writer, artist, scientist, poet, computer expert, business tycoon – indeed in any field of the endless manifestations of what we humans are capable. Even though these accomplishments may be driven by fear, indeed, sometimes terror of invisibility, and are a powerful unconscious means of gaining protective attention, nonetheless the rest of us can enjoy and benefit from these pursuits, and when we are conscious, have compassion for those individuals' inner torment. My hope is that at some point they will encounter the psychological safety so that they themselves will begin to move from fearfulness to fearlessness, from surviving to thriving and leading their precious lives from the inside-out. When the latter inner-determined shifts occur, they will automatically begin to engage their limitless passions as creative play rather than as means of Self-validation.

Psychological safety is where there is the predictable and consistent presence of unconditional love for Self and the other and belief in Self and in the other. There is also the accompaniment of Self where you are at and accompaniment of the other where the other is at – accompaniment with no judgment or imposition or hidden agenda. Only what you consciously experience within Self can you truly express for another. The person who dedicates her life to others is unconsciously dead to Self and to the others for whom she is ceaselessly there – but not really there. In the same way that genius may be unconscious or conscious, so too love can be veiled or openly expressed. Indeed, what is frequently missed is that veiled love of Self – for example, "I feel nothing for myself" – is an act of love. Its protective purpose is to reduce the possibilities of further rejection. If genius is always present – in a hidden or open way – so is love always present. In other words, we cannot but be loving.

The greater the threats to our presence, the more powerful are the protectors – lovingly, knowingly and unconsciously created. No matter how terrifying are the protective responses – to children, adults, partners, pupils, employees – be assured there is always a story to match the intensity of the protectors. Any hint of judgment – a protector in itself – poses a threat and no shift from unconscious to conscious loving and from unconscious to conscious genius expression of your power beyond measure will emerge. Your inner knowing will ensure these processes. When psychological safety is patiently and predictably present, inevitably the inner psychological creative move to conscious expression of love and genius will gradually emerge.

The foregoing is intended to lay the foundations of the book which covers the following:

- A vision of what it means to express conscious genius
- An outline of how unconscious genius manifests itself
- Unconscious psychological safeguarding parenting/teaching – manifestations and effects on children

- Conscious psychological safety parenting/teaching – manifestations and benefits for children
- Unconscious psychological safeguarding leadership/management – manifestations and effects on employees
- Conscious psychological safety leadership/management – manifestations and effects on employees
- The depth and breadth of creating psychological safety
- Psychological safety relationships in homes
- Psychological safety relationships in schools and classrooms
- Psychological safety relationships in workplaces
- Beyond psychological safety

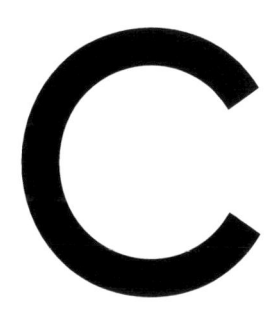

Chapter One:
Radiant Mind

Toddlers mesmerise me with their 'radiant mind' manifesting in excitement, 'wow' responses, endless energy, eagerness to explore and not being fazed by failure or success – the pursuit is reward enough. When children's radiant minds are accompanied and not interrupted by the unconsciously formed fears, doubts, insecurities, depression, impatience, irritability, perfectionism, projections and introjections of the significant adults in their lives – 'feeble mentality' – they continue to shine and conscious genius thrives. Where interruptions occur radiance wisely creates safeguarding fear and now goes into unconscious survival mode, but nonetheless brilliantly. As mentioned in the introduction, Freud missed the reality that the 'feeble mentality' of adults is created wonderfully by radiant mind to offset or reduce the threats they experienced as children. It is in this sense that human suffering is generational and not genetic; it is also a path into what lies hidden of our radiant nature.

The early relationships then that most influence how children will manifest their genius are clearly those in the home, community and school. The nature of these adult-child relationships can be unconsciously or consciously driven and can vary from being terrifying to being loving and inspirational. Later on, when children progress into sports organisations, peer relationships, second-level and third-level educational institutions and workplaces, they will bring either their unconsciously devised psychological safeguarding protectors or conscious psychological safety expressions of their radiant mind. The hope is that there will be adults who are operating consciously who will detect those young people who are suffering and ingeniously surviving and create the psychological safety holding for them so that the possibility of a shift from unconscious psychological safeguarding to conscious psychological safety can occur.

It is how people relate to each other that matters most – parent to child, husband to wife, child to child, teacher to student, peer to peer, doctor to patient, care professional to client and employer to employee. Where the pairing is two adults it is a two-way relationship street. Where it is a child or teenager it is the adult who is largely in the driving seat and young people wisely conform or rebel when the relationship proves to be threatening in nature; they create an internal psychological safeguarding in response to the threats experienced.

As Freud's observations quoted above highlight clearly, the precarious home, school and community relationships that many children encounter are the sources of their unconscious ways of reducing/minimising the threats experienced. Of course, parents and teachers have their stories of their experiences in their homes or origin and schools attended and, unconsciously and ingeniously, carry their psychologically created fears and terrors from those years into adulthood. When they have not been fortunate to experience psychological safety outside their home – most particularly, in schools, in community and workplace – they unconsciously and cleverly maintain the amazing protectors they created when they were children. When adult, their children, their partners, work colleagues and relatives will encounter these solutions to suffering, and when there is psychological safety holding and compassion present will, unconsciously, creatively counter with protectors of their own. The latter outcome will continue to cascade down through the generations until the emergence of psychological safety. No one wants to stay hiding behind the psychological safeguarding walls they ingeniously built in order to survive. However, trust builds slowly when the most important people in your life, sadly for you and for them, were not in a conscious place to wonder at and accompany your unique presence and genius in this world. Nonetheless, I believe, we constantly stay alert to signs of psychological safety.

I will describe in the following chapters what unsafe relationships look like in the various holding worlds we occupy throughout our lives. I will also describe the ultimate psychological safety environment where you will meet the stranger who was yourself, inhabit the I-land that is you and consciously create boundaries as opposed to protectors that uphold your presence and your own values and beliefs in the face of any unconscious attempts by others to invade your I-land. You can only provide psychological safety holding for others when you possess such a safety holding of yourself. Indeed, you can only offer the other the possibility of creating a conscious psychological safety holding to the level of holding you possess in yourself. This is true for all adults no matter what their roles in life are. In the spirit of John Welwood (2000):

> "Not knowing in our blood and bones that we are truly loved and loveable wisely leads us to hide our capacity to give and receive love. This is the core trauma that generates intrapersonal and interpersonal conflict."

It is individuals who principally create relationships and the key psychological safety for others is how you internally relate to yourself:

- Unconditional love of Self
- Belief in Self
- Interest in Self
- Inhabiting your own individuality
- Following your own inner course
- Creating endless opportunities
- Encouragement – giving heart to Self
- Proactive – clear boundaries and independence
- Embracing failures as opportunities
- Responding to success as a stepping stone to further progression
- Separateness from others
- Being at one with Self (al-one-ness)
- No measure of your worth – immeasurable
- Lived experience as the key informant
- Identifying your own passions
- Patient
- Conscious
- Honest

When the above profile is consciously and actively present, then how you are with yourself you will automatically be that way with another and whoever. It reminds me of several individuals who sought help from me, and who, subsequently, in a planned attempt to take their own lives, found their suicide plan interrupted by the felt experience: "Tony loves me… and yes, I can see it in his eyes."

The relationship that needs most attention is the relationship with Self. In my work with individuals and groups I express my own conviction that when you experience the psychological safety to relate consciously with yourself and make that relationship a priority, then you will relate to others in similar ways. Far from being a selfish ambition, the conscious relationship with Self is profoundly unselfish, as you take total responsibility for your own wellbeing and in living your own individual life. There is no unconscious agenda to look to others to save or rescue you, or, indeed, for you to mend the lives of others. In occupying the I-land of your own life, you model, support and create the psychological safety opportunities for others to consciously inhabit their own individuality and live their own unique lives – step by step. Patience is a conscious requirement and echoed so well in D. W. Winnicott's realisation: "I will patiently wait, for an eternity, for you to become present to your life." Indeed, the shift from unconsciousness to consciousness and surviving to thriving is a long journey, beset with many and often more of the threats that originally sent you ingeniously and unconsciously into hiding.

I believe when we see the unconscious genius in people's fears, depression, delusion, paranoia, addictions, compulsions, obsessions, aggression, passivity, violence and in physical illnesses, the therapeutic approach to 'treating' these manifestations of suffering will radically change. Already, there are currently significant signs of such a shift in perspectives both within the psychosocial/psychiatric (Davies, 2013) and medical (Leader, 2008) professions. Narrative psychiatry and medicine are slowly and surely emerging (Schore, 2012).

Staying on the conscious heroic journey of finding psychological safety is greatly helped by having fellow travellers – be they wellbeing practitioners, friends, colleagues, life partners, whoever. The reality is that any one person's relationship with another, be it child, partner, parent, sibling, colleague, friend, can never be greater than the relationship one has with Self. What is unconscious (hidden) is transmitted to the other and the other's unconscious response may remain a continuing block to a fuller life. Equally, when what is conscious is transmitted to the other it opens the doorway to a life fully lived.

In my own therapeutic practice, I am constantly in awe of each person's unique presence and also how he or she found either psychological safety ways or safeguarding ways to express and maintain their individuality in the nurturing or threatening environments of home, school and community.

When there is a family reunion of adult members you could swear that you are hearing about, say, five different families, and you are! From the foregoing, individuality plays a large part in how each person employs their ever-present genius. A common phenomenon is children going opposite ways to each other, wisely not competing, and finding very different characteristics, interests and hobbies. These unconscious developments are an attempt by each child to get seen for their unique presence or, at least, for being different in their behaviour.

I am a twin myself and if I was always at home, my twin was always out; if he was the joker and charmer, I was the shy and serious one; if he was street smart, I was school smart; if I became the minder and carer in the family, he looked to others to mind and care for him, and there were many other differences. What is pertinent here in terms of enduring genius is how individuality is a strong factor in how each person expresses that power beyond measure and that, in spite of what can be unfavourable comparisons, all expressions are equally ingenious. Indeed, in a world of individuals it makes no sense to compare!

It is crucial too that genius is not depersonalised, as if it has a life of its own. As indicated, each human being is an individual – incomparable – and this distinct identity, apart from family name and country of origin, cleverly plays itself out no matter who you are with, where you are, what you are doing and what others are saying or doing. It is the 'I', the Self is the author of all unconscious and conscious ingenious actions.

The following quote by Martin Buber (1878-1965) captures the unique essence of each person:

> "Every person born into this world represents something new, something that never existed before, something original and unique. It is the duty of every person to know and consider that there has never been anyone like him in the world, for if there had been someone like him there would have been no need for him to be in the world. Every single person is a new thing in this world and is called upon to fulfil his particularity in this world. Every person's foremost task is the actualisation of his unique, unprecedented and never-recurring potentialities, and not the repetition of something that another, be it even the greatest, has already achieved."

The inner conscious journey is no less heroic than the unconscious one travelled which was developed in response to threats to your wellbeing and the conscious creations emerge as your experiences of psychological safety flourishes. These creative and heroic psychological safe journeys are illustrated below: Hero's Unconscious Safeguarding Journey 1 – left column, Innate

Psychological Safety Qualities and right column, Unconscious Psychological Safeguarding Creations; Hero's Conscious Psychological Safety Journey 2 – left column, Unconscious Creations and right column, Conscious Qualities.

HERO'S UNCONSCIOUS PSYCHOLOGICAL SAFEGUARDING JOURNEY 1

Innate Psychological Safety Qualities	*Unconscious Psychological Safeguarding Creations*
Radiance	Feebleness
Emerging	Hiding
Spontaneity	Tentativeness
Fearlessness	Fearfulness
Affectionate	Emotional withdrawal
Expression	Repression
Independence	Dependence
Risk-taking	Helplessness
Bridges	Walls
Living	Surviving
Presence	Absence
Inside-out	Outside-in
Connection	Disconnection
Visibility	Invisibility
Expression	Depression

HERO'S CONSCIOUS PSYCHOLOGICAL SAFETY JOURNEY 2

Unconscious Psychological Safeguarding Creations	*Conscious Psychological Safety Qualities*
Anxiety	Radiant mind
Hiding	Emerging
Walls	Bridges
Dependence	Independence
Fearfulness	Fearlessness
Depression	Expression
Surviving	Living
Absence	Presence
Hopelessness	Hopefulness
Liberalism	Symbolism
Outside-in	Inside-out
Disconnection	Connection
Connection	Disconnection
Invisibility	Visibility
Protectors	Boundaries

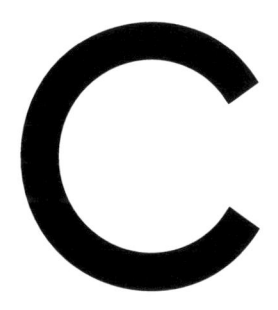

Chapter Two:
Radiant Start

- Everyone is a Genius
- Conscious Psychological Safety Parenting
  - Love of and Excitement Around Learning
  - Enduring Unconditional Love for Self and Children
  - Continuous Natural Curiosity and Excitement About Learning
  - Conversations with Self and Children
  - A Love of Reading and Reading to the Child Early and Often
  - Parents' Expression of Belief in Their Own and the Child's Genius
  - Manifestation of Encouraging Responses to Their Own and the Child's Genius
  - Seeing the Attainment in Every Failure
  - Creating Learning Opportunities for Self and Children

- Patience, Patience, Patience
- Knowing Their Own and the Child's Heroism
- Accompanying Their Own and the Child's Emerging Talents

Everyone is a genius

When I taught primary and secondary school students in the 1970s, I went along with the prevailing (scientifically unsubstantiated) assumption that children are born with different levels of intelligence and some are born with special talents. Much to my regret, acting on that assumption I would have categorised children as slow, dull, average, above average, bright, very bright or genius, depending on how well they performed in class. In the same way, I would have seen some children as having inborn talents and considered them as being genetically lucky compared to their peers who exhibited, in my view, no talent. Later on, as a psychology student, I was trained to administer various Intelligence Tests, most notably the WISC (Wechsler Intelligence Scale for Children) and the WAIS (Wechsler Adult Intelligence Scale). On these latter tests, scores ranged from:

0-29 Severely disadvantaged

30-49 Moderately disadvantaged

50-69 Mildly disadvantaged

70-89 Dull

90-109 Average

110-119 Bright

120-129 Superior

130-139 Very superior

140+ Genius

On completion of my PhD in Clinical Psychology, I began to work in psychiatric hospitals where I was often requested to carry out IQ tests on individuals referred by psychiatrists. But, by then, I had ceased to believe in the notion that individuals are born with different levels of intelligence and, indeed, that there were any genetic or biological bases to psychiatric diagnoses such as schizophrenia, bi-polar depression or personality disorder. I had also come seriously to doubt the value of the widespread labelling of children that was then, and still is, prevalent – labels such as ADD (attention deficit disorder), ADHD (attention deficit, hyperactive disorder), dyspraxia, dyslexia, autism, ODD (oppositional defiance disorder). What had become clear to me in assessing adults' and children's intelligence and psychosocial functioning was that no account was being taken of individual life-stories and how the environment to which individuals are exposed impacts on their overall functioning.

What I found particularly maddening was the absence of scientific evidence to support the labels used, and the conclusion that these labels represented 'incurable' conditions. Davies (2013) in his evidenced-based examination of the history of psychiatry found that "after nearly 50 years of investigation into the chemical imbalance theory, there is not one piece of convincing evidence that the theory is actually correct." What emerged for me was that the DSM (Diagnostic and Statistical Manual of Mental Disorders) was essentially a book of fiction. In my therapeutic work with children and adults what I was discovering was their genius and their talent in finding ways of surviving what often were very threatening environments in their homes, schools and communities.

These individuals, far from being dysfunctional, were heroes and heroines. The threatening psychosocial, and sometimes physical, relationships were created by the significant adults in their lives who, unconsciously, were living from their unresolved fears, fears which in turn arose from the threats they had encountered in their earlier and current lives.

The reality is that unless individuals find the psychological safety within to bring to consciousness their deep-seated fears and depressions, these will endlessly repeat; as already mentioned, human misery is not genetic but it is generational. During the ten years I worked in psychiatric settings I refused to carry out any tests on any individuals, and neither was I prepared to require any individuals to complete commonly employed inventories such as those apparently concerned with depression, anxiety or obsessive-compulsive behaviour. My approach was to create a relationship with the individual – whether adult, adolescent or child – to explore their individual stories with them, and begin together to bring into consciousness the 'unsayables' and the 'undoables', the hidden traumas and treasures of their being, and their multiple unmet needs.

Love and patience proved to be essential, as was awe, not only in the face of each person's unique presence, but in the face of how ingeniously and creatively each had found ways to survive the slings and arrows of outrageous misfortune. There was no lack of intelligence or talent present; on the contrary, it was evident that enormous resources had been employed to manage the unconscious protective behaviours they had encountered in the relationships with parents, carers and teachers. Not surprisingly, many deeply distressed individuals wanted to see me and their therapeutic progress was a source of amazement and confusion to my professional colleagues, such that a whisper going around the hospital and community was "What does he do?" Freud, in a letter to Carl Jung, captured something of what I was doing when he wrote: "We cure people with love." Cure is not a word I use because it suggests illness or dysfunction. Protectors are not problems, they are necessary psychological creations in the face of threats to your wellbeing, walls you create to hide behind until it becomes emotionally safe to emerge.

In working with children, it is the adults who have been the unwitting source of the children's traumas who need to be the main focus of co-creational interventions. Certainly, with children who have been deeply traumatised, contact with an appropriate healthcare professional is also necessary because it is in that relationship the child may begin to trust again. When it comes to individuals in their late teens, supporting them to become independent is important, as well as working with those adults who, unconsciously, had darkened their presence. In my work with adults, creating a relationship of unconditional love, belief in them, non-judgment and expressed wonder at their survival skills is essential.

In terms of intelligence, as outlined in the Introduction, there is now evidence that all children are born with immense intellectual potential, and it is the environment to which they are exposed and, most of all, each child's creative response to those outside factors – emotional, sexual, physical, behavioural, intellectual, social and creative – that determine how the child's giftedness is employed. Typically, intelligence has been measured by a child's knowledge of school subjects – a very limited range given the many areas of human knowledge and skills – and, too often, the child who does not show achievement in those school subjects is lost and may only blossom when he or she leaves school.

What is now emerging is that a child's genius is *always* present and is being used in ways that best serve him or her in the different holding worlds occupied – womb, home, school, community and country. When a child is not managing to learn a particular school subject, it does not mean he or she has not got the ability to achieve in that particular area – a frequent assumption made by parents and teachers, often resulting in a child being labelled slow or weak or dull or not having academic potential. Nothing is further from the truth, because the potential to learn and be creative in any specific subject or skill is there up to the time you die. The reality that is often not seen is that the child's priorities are elsewhere, in line with what he or she is experiencing, principally in the home environment and often exacerbated in the school environment.

What has not come to consciousness for most educational, psychological, psychiatric and social professionals is that the genius of many children (and, indeed, adults) manifests itself in their unconscious protective responses to the threats they encounter – such as irritability, annoyance, harshness, impatience, comparisons, slapping, sexual violations, unrealistic expectations, enforced practice of knowledge and skills, suffocation of individuality, bullying, overprotection, lack of interest in them, indifference, little or no affection, starvation of belief in them – to name but a few. Certainly, the frequency, intensity and persistence of those threats are a crucial consideration.

The psychological safeguarding strategies children intelligently develop in the face of such behaviours can be emotional withdrawal, emotionlessness, nail-biting, thumb-sucking, being overpleasing, being appeasing, conformity, obsessiveness, rebelliousness, self-harming, refusal to eat, overeating, major separation anxiety, aggression, violence, physical ailments, school refusal, temper tantrums, hatred of school – again to name but a few. Each defence or protector is an act of genius, an attempt by the child to draw attention to the hurts he or she is experiencing and an attempt to reduce the frequency, intensity and endurance of these violations.

The typical unconscious response of most adults to these reactions of children is to see these children as problematic rather than as ingenious, and to label, ignore, medicate, punish and marginalise them. These responses on the part of the adults arise from their own fears, and are their ingenious attempts to manage their own unresolved traumas and the threatening environments in which they live. Again, the unacknowledged reality is that fear dominates most adults' lives – most especially fear of what others think – and leads to them ingeniously and unconsciously creating all manner of protectors to best manage all the threats to their wellbeing.

It is for this reason that it is vital that a culture is developed where it is an accepted reality for all adults – most especially parents, teachers, politicians, psychologists, social workers, medical professionals, psychiatrists, university faculty members, leaders in business and industry – in the words of Socrates to "Know Self and Know the Other". How can any adult inspire children when not living their own life, not putting one's head above the parapet, not daring to express individuality, not daring to be different, to speak the truth, to risk-take, to embrace failure as opportunity, success as a stepping stone, and learning and work as creative play? What a different world we would have where consciousness of our true and powerful nature is predominant.

The inverse of the word *live* is *evil* and there is no greater threat to a child or adult than the message '*do not live your own life*'. An all too common creative protector is where a person either lives life for the other (thereby extinguishing his or her birthright to a life of one's own) or intimidates others to live life for him or her (thereby extinguishing the other's birthright to live life for oneself) or living to work or succeed (thereby cleverly extinguishing one's person in favour of recognition through work and success). There is no wrong here, only ingenuity. However, when our genius is unconsciously and necessarily creatively employed to use our amazing potential to build walls to hide behind, then everybody loses. When the ingenuity of our protective responses is universally acknowledged, this will herald an unprecedented shift in how we live, parent, educate, work, pray, play, manage and lead.

I recall a primary school teacher approaching me about a child in her classroom, aged 10 at the time, whom she described as "a reincarnated American genius". The child was streets ahead of the other children in terms of knowledge of the different school subjects; indeed, he frequently knew more than the teacher herself. She decided to have the child assessed by an educational psychologist. The psychologist used the WISC to determine, as he saw it, the child's intelligence and the child achieved an IQ score of 148. When the psychologist was communicating the result to the teacher, he told her that she had "a genius in her classroom".

I expressed curiosity regarding the psychologist's view on the child's American accent, and also about the facts that the child did not mix with other children, did not engage in games, and was noticeably emotionally unexpressive. The psychologist's response was "That goes with being a genius." There was no attempt to enquire about the child's story to date, and how it could have come about that a child who lived in a quintessentially Irish rural area, with parents who had themselves been reared in the same area, had developed a marked American accent. When I enquired about the child's home environment, I discovered that his mother, who had high educational ambitions for her first-born, had exposed him to American educational videotapes from very early on in his life, and that was how the child had developed his accent. His mother was also very occupationally driven and a perfectionist in everything she did in the home and at work. The child's father worked in another county and came home only at weekends. He was very passive and emotionally withdrawn. The boy had ingeniously conformed to his mother's expectations and so was achieving very highly educationally. However, socially and emotionally he was far behind his peers and his isolation from them was beginning to take its toll.

Where children show remarkable educational knowledge but little emotional and social development, there is no genetic or biological evidence for the presence of these deficits. Actually, what is evident is that these deficits have arisen from these children's ingenious responses to their troubled environments and that considerable intervention is required with the parents and the teachers to redeem their inner psychological safety and provide the opportunities for the children to apply their intelligence to the development of these absent essential skills. This can be a slow process because the unique presence of emotional and social expressiveness and receptivity in the children, the parents and the teachers have long lain dormant. When it comes to understanding and helping children, it is parents and teachers *first*, then children.

Interestingly, in the case of the 'reincarnated genius' there was a younger brother who was regarded as a 'dunce' in the same school where his brother was regarded as a genius. Nobody saw that the younger brother's genius lay in going the opposite way to his brother – how could he ever compete with him? Sadly, this child was an embarrassment to his mother, but he did creatively find a way to get some attention from her by being frequently sick. Where each child is, is where each child needs to be. This is also true for adults. When inner psychological safety is consistently and predictably present, and trust slowly but surely is found, the same genius that created the walls shifts to creating bridges and gradually fearfulness is replaced with fearlessness, reticence with risk-taking, hiding with emerging, repression with expression, conformity with individuality, incarceration with freedom and Self-realisation through inhabiting one's unique presence and not visibility through achievements. Indeed, when the latter is present, learning becomes a conscious pursuit.

Conscious psychological safety parenting

Each child is a genius and has the endless potential to become talented in knowledge and skills for which he or she shows passion. What is essential is that in the child's exploration of what he or she encounters no threat occurs, so that ingenuity stays with the excitement of learning and is not needed to create protectors around any threats experienced. The first three years are crucial, and parents and child-minders are the first teachers. Parents and child-minders deserve to have the opportunities to examine how they feel around their intelligence, because if they are still unconsciously carrying diminishing labels in regard to their intellectual functioning it is inevitable that they will project how they see themselves on to the child. Possibilities here are low expectations, unrealistic expectations, non-involvement with the child's eagerness to learn, perfectionism, impatience, comparisons and lack of belief in the child's wonderful potential.

Parents can bring their children only to where they are themselves. Bringing a child into the world often calls for the parents to reflect on their lives to this point in time, the nature of their relationships with themselves and others, and their education and career histories to date. It is seldom that parents have consciousness of their genius, even though that genius is always actively present. It is equally rare for teachers to know their individual genius. No wonder then that most of us have suffered under the shadow of that best-kept secret – we are all geniuses! It is certainly a secret that needs to be broadcast and when it is by parents, child-minders and teachers, one of the greatest threats to children consciously maximising their individual potential will be extinguished. When parents struggle with a sense of intellectual and educational inferiority, for their own sakes and their children's sake it is important that unconditional regard and support are available for them from someone who is both a relationship and educational practitioner, so they may explore how they had come to such struggles around realisation of their true ingenious nature and how, unwittingly, they had necessarily employed their genius to survive rather than thrive.

When parents consciously act from their ingenious and creative nature, their children in the presence of the parents' psychological safety holding of their own selves will fearlessly give expression too to their amazing nature. These parents will consciously manifest in their everyday behaviour the following:

- Love of and excitement around learning
- Enduring unconditional love for Self and children
- Continuous natural curiosity and eagerness to learn
- Conversations with Self and child
- A love of reading and reading to the child early and often
- Expression of belief in their own and in the child's genius
- Manifestation of encouraging responses to their own and the child's genius
- Seeing the attainment in every failure
- Creating learning opportunities for Self and child
- Patience, patience, patience
- Knowing their own and the child's heroism
- Accompaniment with their own and the child's emerging talents

As you will see, the presence of each of these factors supports the inner psychological safety of children to manifest what is true of their nature – lovability and ingenuity uninterrupted.

Love of and excitement around learning

A great attraction for pre-school and school-going children is to try out what they see their parents doing. A phrase commonly heard from toddlers is "*I* do, *I* do" in response to some action being carried out by a parent. The conscious parent's response will be "just do it" or "let's do it together", acknowledging whatever is attained. Even when the child fails to manage the action, the conscious parent will convey to the child "I'm so pleased you tried and there will be more opportunities to try again." When children see parents enjoying what they do and not getting upset when things go against them or not going over the top with self-praise when they are successful, they will come to see all learning – not just school learning – as creative play.

Enduring unconditional love for Self and children

This is particularly challenging for parents because the majority will have experienced conditional love relating in their childhood years and, unless they have become conscious of it, they will now be operating that way with themselves and with others. Conscious parents do not confuse their own or the child's unique and sacred person with *any* behaviour. Unconditional love is for the person's – whether child or adult – unique presence. When a child experiences love being tied to 'good' behaviour or any achievement, a wise hidden fear is created that 'if I fail, love will be withdrawn and that possibility is terrifying to me'. Unconsciously and ingeniously, the child will find some safeguarding/protective way to reduce or eliminate this frightening threat. The child may become performance driven, a 'bookworm', overinvolved with the behaviours that gain attention; he or she may begin to refuse to do those very behaviours that gain attention (conditional) because of the potential dangers in doing them; he or she may complain of tummy aches whenever asked to engage in the behaviours – one way or another the child will use his or her genius to survive.

I am reminded of parents who approached me about their 15-year-old daughter who had refused point blank to go to secondary school three years previously. Both parents had high-powered professional jobs and were extremely performance driven. An older daughter studying medicine was their pride and joy, even though she presented with anorexia nervosa when she was 16. In my experience anorexia nervosas metaphorically can represent a starvation of love, which was certainly the case here. Their daughter was medically force-fed but no health professional considered her story and put two and two together. Like her parents, she became highly anxious around examinations and was prescribed anxiolytics for this 'condition'. The sad thing was that nobody spotted the alarming 'conditionality' present.

As regards the younger daughter, the parents had brought her to neurologists in Ireland and abroad, trying to determine what could be neurologically causing their daughter's school refusal. Their unconscious blindness to the conditional nature of their relationship with each daughter arose from the fact that they were just as conditional with themselves. Their psychological safeguarding was to covertly get recognition through their academic and professional successes and any consciousness of how they were with their daughter would mean facing into the pain of their own abandonment experiences around school-work when they were children. Ingeniously, they needed to hold fast to their dependence on outside recognition until they experienced a relationship where no threat to their presence existed.

The younger daughter and I co-created a solid relationship and she gradually became conscious of her remarkable protective strategies and the gradual realisation 'I'm not an examination result'. Her parents witnessed an emergence of more emotional contact with them and an inclination to socialise more with her peers. They eventually attended for themselves and their subsequent realisations considerably supported their daughter's emancipation.

The daughter and I kept up occasional contact over the years, and when she was in her early 20s she decided to attend university, not to prove herself to her parents or to herself but to enjoy the adventure of learning.

Continuous natural curiosity and excitement about learning

Not only is a child's person deserving of a 'wow' response but so is their genius and their need to excitedly explore. Accompanying a child's curiosity and excitement around learning is vital to nurturing real expression of these wonderful natural gifts. The psychological safety parent is patient, encouraging, exciting and accompanies at the child's pace – as it is for themselves. Adults often have the urge to hurry children along, but this is an adult imposing their own need to complete a task and can result in demotivating the child. Parents who model natural curiosity and excitement around learning are alert around non-verbal behaviours: tone of voice, body posture, eye contact, nature of touch, breath and concentration. Verbally, they enquire how the child is feeling with what he or she is exploring. They know that it is their attention that ensures the child will stay on task; the contrary is also true.

Conversations with Self and children

There is considerable research indicating that one-to-one talking with a child provides a powerful supportive start to language development. Not surprisingly, the child who has benefited from these conversations can be a teacher's 'dream child'. The child's articulation can be quite sophisticated and the teacher's nurturing of this language skill adds sizeably to the work that the parents have done. Whilst this child has a head-start on the particular subject nurtured, it does not mean that other children who have not had such a fortunate start do not have the capability to catch up – they decidedly do! Once these young people experience not being criticised, compared, marginalised, labelled, or medicated, they will thrive under the individualised championing of their amazing ability to learn – anything.

One swallow does not make a summer, and it takes considerable ongoing efforts on the part of the parents, child-minders and teachers to have conscious conversations with themselves around their own amazing potential and from these engage in conversations with the young person – an experience the child will always treasure. The degree to which the parent and other significant adults come into conscious acknowledgement of their own undeniable genius will continue to determine the conversations they will have with their young charges.

A love of reading and reading to the child early and often

Children love their parents to read with them. Naturally, they want the parent to read "just one more page, please". What is crucial here is the emotional contact, particularly if due to being busy with household and other tasks it has been largely absent during the day. In other words, the company of the parent is more important than the reading with them. Nevertheless, as for speaking with children, reading with children adds hugely to their language proficiency and their reading ability. Again, *how* it is done is important – fun being an essential ingredient. Of course, parents need their own space to read and explore, and when children plead for "just five more minutes" the parent can kindly say "I'd love to read you more, but I need some time for myself now" and then follow through with action, lovingly leaving the room. Boundaries are evidence of adult psychological safety, and when there is some time for reading as well as solitude for parents and couple contact, this means that everybody gains.

Parents' expression of belief in their own and the child's genius

I will always remember a teenager saying to me "Tony, belief is everything." I replied that "I feel love comes first and that, yes, belief certainly comes second." The interesting fact is that confidence is natural to infants and toddlers and only begins to go underground when children encounter not only the absence of expressed belief in them but the threatening tone of voice, the 'look that kills', the cold dismissal, and the lack of interest in their explorations. How can these adults, whose behaviours so threaten the child's presence and ingenious expression, communicate absolute belief in the child; they cannot do so until they unearth what they had had to wisely bury when they themselves were children.

The genius and psychological safeguarding in adults being 'feeble-minded' or aggressive is that they effectively get others to stop asking them to do things or answer questions or take on new challenges, thereby eliminating failure, impatience, irritability, aggression and other threats. Unless these adults are provided with opportunities to come into a psychological safety holding of their individuality and power beyond measure, inevitably their children's radiance will be shadowed. When adults – especially parents and teachers – truly believe in and give expression to that belief in themselves and in their children, then children thrive intellectually, behaviourally, socially, emotionally and educationally. When adults thrive, children thrive; when adults survive, children survive!

Manifestation of encouraging responses to their own and the child's genius

I remember while waiting for a flight at Zurich airport noticing a family of three – parents and a child probably three or four years old. It was clear they were rushing to catch a flight, and the parents in their hurry were striding out quickly. The child who had his own knapsack on his back was valiantly trying to keep up but was not able to match his parents' pace. The father turned around and crossly said "Come on, come on, you have to hurry up." The child did his best to lengthen his stride but it was not good enough. The father stopped and with obvious exasperation took the knapsack from the child's back, picked him up and began to carry him. The child shrieked and I wondered how many of the observers saw the full story.

Of course, the father was anxious to make the flight but he failed to see the brave efforts of the little fellow to carry his own luggage and to try to keep up with his very tall father. When the father sternly requested the child to "come on, come on", if instead he had taken him by the hand and said "let's run together for the plane" there is no doubt his son would have beamed up at him. Equally, when he displayed much annoyance and took the child's bag and picked him up, if, instead, he had stooped down to his son's eye level and said "come on, climb on my back and we'll get to the plane together", again there is no doubt that his son would have eagerly cooperated. It was the father's tone of voice and the humiliation of being publicly criticised that hugely upset the child.

The word courage comes from the French word *coeur* (heart) and encouragement is to give heart to one's own and the child's efforts in learning any skill. It is best if encouragement is specific. Telling a child he or she is the greatest child for doing homework is not being specific and is tying affection to tasks. In the story above, the psychological safety parent could have communicated to the child "thank you for carrying your own bag" and "look how well you have been trying to keep up with your Mum and Dad". The secret is to aim encouragement at the task the child is engaged in; for example, "I like how you tidy your toys away after playing, thank you"; "how you concentrate on your schoolwork is impressive"; "I know that was a difficult task to do, but I like how you stayed with it and completed it." Conscious psychological safety parents know that love is for the person of the child and praise and encouragement are for specific behaviours – real magic!

Seeing the attainment in every failure

A very common tendency among adults when responding to their own or a child's learning efforts or explorations is to focus on the performance rather than the attainment. A performance response sees an action as right or wrong and can result in either the adult or the child wanting to 'always get it right' or avoidance of making the effort to practise – both ingenious protective reactions designed to reduce criticism. Consciously seeing the attainment maintains the inner drive to learn. For example, when a small child is attempting to speak a new word – let us say "ball" – the very attempt itself is an attainment and the conscious adult will reflect that attainment. The second attainment is in the attempted enunciation – for example, the child says "ba" – the child is halfway there and again the parent's response will reflect that – "yes, magic, say it again, ball." The crucial issue here is that no hint of criticism is present. Children are experts at picking up disapproval, particularly from facial expression, body posture and tone of voice. An unconscious performance-driven teaching in homes, pre-schools, primary and second-level schools, and further in higher education settings takes the heart out of learning. Attainment-driven learning and teaching maintain the natural love and pursuit of knowledge and skills.

Creating learning opportunities for Self and children

Toddlers become wide-eyed with excitement when exposed to different learning opportunities. I recall being on the top floor of a contemporary university building when the glass doors of the lift opened and a father and child not more than three years of age stepped out of the lift and the child's response was "Wow" to the architectural delight of being on the top floor and being able to see all the way down to the ground floor. Very often, due to early hurts experienced around learning, we have lost that 'wow' response, and unless we resurrect it, it is unlikely we will nurture it in children.

Certainly, being with young children may touch into that hidden 'wow' and such an experience is a shift in consciousness for the adult and an important bonus for the child. There are no prescriptions here – parents are where they need to be, never consciously wanting to burst the child's excitement balloon – but even being reminded of the 'wow' experience may awaken what has been dormant for the adult. Certainly, the more learning opportunities a child receives – words, feelings, actions, play, reading, people, places, games, skills – the more the child will thrive in a range of ways. Equally, the more parents and other significant adults in children's lives fearlessly seek out learning opportunities, the more children will do likewise.

Patience, patience, patience

Patience – easier said than done! You can be preoccupied with responsibilities, tired, busy, burdened with cares, anxious, depressed, and staying patient with a child's energetic behaviour requires a fair degree of conscious governorship of Self. Like every other way you need to be with another – child or adult – it always starts with yourself. It is you who deserves patience to be there for yourself and, when patience is there for you, it will spontaneously be there for another. Parents carry many responsibilities, the most important being the care of Self. There is nothing more unselfish than love and care of yourself, because it means you take complete responsibility for your own life and do not unconsciously pass the buck of responsibility on to another – be it parent on to child, spouse on to spouse, teacher on to pupil, friend on to friend, employer on to employee.

The secret plea often is 'mend my life'. Conscious psychological safety is the realisation that only you now as an adult can save your life. As a child, you needed parents to be there for you and to slowly and in an age-related and patient manner to pass responsibility for your life on to yourself. Here-and-now consciously embracing your own life will ensure consciousness of the privileged responsibility to be there for your child. Patience emerges as you deepen your consciousness of taking charge of your presence and destiny and maintaining your integrity and dignity in the face of other individuals' protective behaviours.

When you lose patience with a child, it is not the child's behaviour that causes it but some care of yourself that is absent, and your impatience is alerting you to that reality. The possibilities are endless – tiredness, doing too much, rarely or ever asking for help or support, perfectionism, fear of getting it wrong, fear of how others may see you, not putting yourself first – only you know the answer.

Everyone loses patience, because there are few of us who are totally there for ourselves. At least, when you are conscious that your impatience is of you, belongs to you and is for you, you can apologise to the child and explain the source of the impatience. For example, "Mummy wasn't looking after herself and I'm sorry I took that out on you. Let me give you a hug."

Clearly, the importance of patience is that it provides a predictable and consistent supportive holding for the child so that neither the child's presence nor natural curiosity and eagerness to learn are interrupted. Again, the odd burst of impatience is redeemable; it is the frequency, endurance over time and intensity that pose the greatest threats.

Knowing their own and the child's heroism

It is a pleasure to witness a child looking up to a parent as Hero/Heroine and wanting to be a hero/heroine too. We are always heroic – either unconsciously (protectively/fearfully) or consciously (fearlessly). It is in being a conscious hero/heroine that you inspire your child – showing your dare-devil side, your championing of Self and the child, your fearlessness, spontaneity, your love of learning, your particular passions, your determination, persistence, seizing failure as opportunity and success as a stepping stone to more knowledge and skills, your aliveness, your energy, your freedom, independence, integrity and genuineness – what a hero/heroine!

Furthermore, what contributes hugely to children becoming fearlessly creative is when allowed to explore their own beliefs and values and discover their own interests.

Accompanying their own and the child's emerging talents

Like intelligence, talents are not inborn and, contrary to what many people believe, there are no born musicians, footballers, mathematicians, artists, scientists. The research shows that what has been called giftedness is a gradual development of skills over a period of time. So-called 'gifted' children rarely thrive in adulthood, primarily due to being performance-driven, being seen for their achievements rather than for themselves, and affection being tied to the area of knowledge or skill that has gained them undue attention from parents and teachers. Every adult and child has the potential to become talented and, particularly, in behaviours that they are energised and passionate about.

When parents accompany their own and the child's passionate pursuits and do not confuse the person with the pursuits, they can nurture emerging talents in several ways. Staying emotionally attuned both with their own and the child's excitement, attainments and disappointments will certainly help. Continual exposure to opportunities to engage with the particular passion, provision of exceptional and patient instruction, encouragement of practice, and frequently accompanying the child in his or her practice are further building blocks to the conscious creative process.

Be assured that each child is exceptional, individual and different and with modelling by the significant adults in his or her life and no unconscious projection of unmet needs by them on to the child's achievements, then anything is possible. There is no greater reward in learning than the satisfaction in little attainments experienced in the pursuit of a passion – external rewarding extinguishes passion. Individuals are born to live their own lives, not the lives of their parents or teachers. When the latter happens, the development of conscious talents is seriously interrupted – unintentionally!

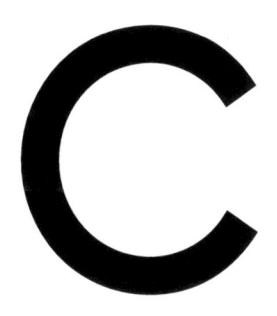

Chapter Three:
Psychological Safeguarding

- Children are Creative, not Hard-wired
- The Story Behind What Adults Do
- Adults Never Stop Talking About Themselves
- What Arises in Adults is About the Adults!
- Children's Psychological Safeguarding

Children are creative, not hard-wired

In the light of evidence that the early years in a child's life affect the child's later potential in emotional wellbeing, physical health, education and employment, there is an urgent need to transform psychological and social services for parents and children, espccially in the first three years of life. There is now a growing political realisation that children who are traumatised create very significant costs. It is now realised that the financial costs pale in comparison to the emotional costs to the child's sense of Self. Another belief often expressed is that children who experience neglect, physical and sexual abuse or emotional abandonment become 'hard-wired' in their responses to the neglect experienced – for example, aggression, withdrawal, depression, anxiety and insecurity, learning difficulties and physical ailments.

Similarly, there is a belief that children who receive 'good enough' parenting – conscious and loving support, and a predictable and consistent environment – become 'hard-wired' to expect security, care and love. This term 'hard-wired', though it has a ring of science, is, in fact, meaningless; it also fails to recognise the ever-present genius and creativity of both children and adults. Another message frequently voiced is that the most critical aspect of the infant's life is the relationship between infant and key carer – usually the mother.

A number of concerns arise in regard to the foregoing messages. One concern is about once again putting all the responsibility for the conscious psychological safety rearing of a child on the mother's shoulders, and not at all emphasising that when a child does not experience a caring relationship with the father, the child may well wisely close off from reaching out to males. Furthermore, it takes the world to raise a child and each adult who interacts with a child affects how that child sees himself or herself. The latter view is supported by the story of a three-year-old child who had received a gift in the post from her grandfather and, when requested to send a thank-you card, had asserted strongly "No, I won't, he never looks at me and never speaks to me!"

A similar story concerns a young man who is terrified in the company of women – "my mother was scary" he exclaimed – but is comfortable in the company of men – "my father was kind though passive." Yet another story is of a teenager whose parents had unconsciously abandoned him, who displayed major aggression towards teachers, both male and female, except with one male teacher who befriended him and was kind and supportive.

In formulating approaches to the rearing and teaching of children, it is vital that all adults who are likely to encounter children are provided with psychological safety opportunities to examine their own lives and to develop consciousness of their own and each child's unique presence and unconditional lovability and capability. It is rarely acknowledged that the relationship that parents and other significant adults in children's lives have with themselves determines how they relate to children, and when protective in nature, it is unconsciously driven. It is important to emphasise that all parenting starts with the parents themselves, all teaching starts with the teachers themselves, all healthcare starts with the healthcare providers, all management starts with the managers themselves and all leadership starts with the leaders themselves. Loving and empowering ways of rearing children can only be present when the adults involved are that way in their own relationship with themselves or, at least, coming into consciousness and practice of it.

The greatest concern arises from the notion that children become 'hard-wired' in their reactions to abandonment experiences and are subsequently viewed as 'dysfunctional'. It is curious that Alan Schore (2012) describes a child's responses to threats to wellbeing as being *adaptive* when they first occur, but in later years these responses are seen as pathological *disorders*. The more common *disorders* with which children are labelled are ADD, ADHD, ODD, dyspraxia, dyslexia and autism. Currently, some three and a quarter million children are labelled with ADHD in America, and about 2.5% of all-American children are labelled as bi-polar depressed and are on antidepressant medication. In Ireland, one in 65 children are labelled autistic.

My own experience in working with young or older children or teenagers is that when I establish a strong relationship bond the so-called 'hard-wired' psychological safeguarding responses are gradually replaced with receptivity to care and expressions of love and friendship. It is more accurate to say that when children encounter the suffering of adults in their early years they creatively develop powerful ways of psychological safeguarding strategies to manage and reduce hurt, and only at a later point, when they consistently experience love and belief in them, will they again risk trusting that they are indeed lovable and powerful. The 'hard-wired' concept also misses the fact that the psychological safeguarding/ protective responses formed in the early years also serve the creative purpose of acting as a *substitute* for the *real* experience of being loved for Self.

Typical protective behaviours developed are overpleasing, passivity, aggression, illness, perfectionism, being focused on performance, being 'difficult'. All of these unconscious creations get some kind of response from adults and thereby reduce the child's sense of invisibility. If, later on, children experience being loved for themselves, they again employ their intelligence and creativity, but this time these are employed in being openly rather than protectively responsive. Seeing children as dysfunctional and suffering from disorders results in children being abandoned once again, thereby increasing their sense of invisibility, lowering their self-esteem rather than affirming their unique presence and individuality, and their power beyond measure to determine when it is psychologically safe or threatening to be themselves. What is urgent here is that those professionals who label children as 'disordered' deserve the psychological safety to examine the protective sources of their behaviours.

The story behind what adults do

No matter where you are or what you are doing, whether you are alone or with others, you are always in relationship. Typically, we think of relationship in terms of intimate relationship between, for example, parent and child, between friends, lovers or spouses. But different kinds of relationship occur in all the places where we live, learn, work, heal, play and pray, and need just as much attention as the relationships between intimates. Furthermore, each relationship is always a couple relationship, whether it is between a parent and child, two lovers, a manager and employee, a teacher and student, a parishioner and priest, a doctor and patient, a citizen and politician. Any parent, teacher, politician, leader, manager, employer, medical professional or member of the clergy who sees a group as a single entity rather than a collection of individuals unconsciously misses a fundamental and critical issue: each person in that group will respond to him or her in a unique way. In fact, he or she is dealing with a number of couple relationships. If all family members, employees, patients, clients, students are treated in the same way, the creative dynamic of the uniqueness and individuality of each human being is being overlooked. In reality, each child in a particular family has a different mother and a different father, each employee has a different employer, each student in a class has a different teacher, each patient in a particular surgery has a different doctor, and each client in a particular relationship mentoring or psychotherapy practice has a different relationship mentor or psychotherapist.

There is the further reality that each individual has a story that is a unique autobiography, known only by that individual. Some aspects of a person's story may be known only at the unconscious level and this hidden life will become available to consciousness only when the person finds adequate psychological safety, initially with another and, subsequently, within himself or herself.

The story of a person's life is not just the events he or she encounters – for example, a difficult birth, a loving mother, an emotionless home, conditional loving, violent father, kind grandparent or affirming teacher. The story also consists of the person's inner unique and individual responses to such events. It is truly amazing how – whether in families, classrooms or workplaces – each person finds their own particular and creative responses to whatever situation arises. This makes sense because when two individuals interact inevitably their interaction will be of a unique nature. Parents are powerful witnesses to how each child is completely different from his or her siblings, and this is so whether children are raised in benign or difficult circumstances.

Adults reared as children in adverse circumstances will express their individuality through the unconscious formation of a very powerful and unique array of psychological safeguarding behaviours that are designed both to reduce the threats to wellbeing being encountered, and to bring to the attention of any conscious adult who may be around their deeply troubled interior and exterior worlds. Those adults, who as children experienced a stable and loving family, also expressed their individuality through the development of a repertoire of open and psychological safety responses that were different from those of siblings. Adults whose wellbeing in their early years was in daily jeopardy were ingenious in finding ways to repress (hide away) or disassociate (not connect with) those aspects of their true nature that they dared not exhibit, while those whose wellbeing was unconditionally held were ingenious in the ways they expressed and manifested their individuality, ensuring that they were not confused with anyone else in the family.

As adults, that deep inner drive to occupy our own individuality continues, but to respond openly to that drive we need to find the psychological safety to become aware of our unconscious and conscious responses. You may well ask "Are we not always conscious of what we feel, think, say and do?" Certainly, you may notice that you can be aggressive, violent, shy, timid or manipulative at times, but you may not be conscious of the sources and the psychological safeguarding intentions of such protective responses. The common response is to employ other unconscious protectors, such as rationalisation (creating what appear to be 'reasonable' explanations for unreasonable behaviours), denial ("I have no problems"), projection ("everybody else is wrong"), or introjection ("I'm just bad, and I have no control over what I say or do"). Unless the sources are uncovered, the unconsciously formed psychological safeguarding responses, towards Self or towards others, will continue. Outer psychological safety gradually gives rise to conscious inner psychological safety in adults, so that they gradually develop an owning, understanding and accountability for inner and outer protective behaviours, begin to be true to Self to make fearless conscious choices and take fearless conscious actions.

Take the example of the school principal who bullies and intimidates staff members. When confronted he is likely to justify and rationalise his threatening responses by, for example, declaring "nobody would do anything around here without being shouted at" or "being bullied did me no harm as a child." But when that manager compassionately understands the bullying behaviour as an unconscious psychological safeguarding response arising from unresolved fears within himself – for example, fear of failure, fear of what others think, fear of letting down parents – it is likely that a conscious psychological safety will emerge of the real threat that he unwittingly has been posing to the wellbeing of others. Once that inner psychological safety is present, new choices and new actions are now possible towards himself and towards others.

Getting to the story of what led to the bullying is not an attempt to dilute the serious emotional threat that bullying poses; sadly, many suicides are prompted by the experience of being bullied.

On the contrary, getting to the story is a crucial response to the serious threat; unless the person who bullies becomes conscious of his hidden unresolved fears and hurts, his cleverly designed psychological safeguarding behaviour will continue and is likely to escalate when outside pressures increase.

Conscious psychological safety relating is only possible when what lies hidden is brought to the surface and what it was in that story that led to the creative development of bullying as a means of protecting against hurt. Individuals who bully need safety and support to stand with themselves, so that they are no longer dependent on others standing with them – conscious psychological safety. The overt unconscious intention of bullying is to ensure control, but the covert intention is to draw attention to the urgent need to be in control of Self and to support others to do likewise.

Whatever threatening behaviours adults may engage in, towards themselves or others, the unravelling of their purpose can be found only in the examination of story and the discovery of what the protective responses are doing for them in a hidden way that they dare not do openly.

Adults never stop talking about themselves

One of the biggest conscious revelations facing us as adults is to own the fact that no matter what we say we are always talking about ourselves! For unconscious reasons, this truth is often a bitter pill to swallow. We tend to carry the illusion that what I say is about the other and that what the other says is about me; for example, I say "You're always late" and think that what I'm saying is a straightforward statement about the other's tardiness. But the question is: "How come I'm making that statement, what has the other's tardiness got to do with me?" and why am I not saying what I'm really feeling? The answer likely to emerge is that "I'm feeling angry and frustrated at having to wait around every time you're late." Furthermore, the question arises as to what underlies my waiting? Is it not the case that I am being tardy in the care of myself and in setting a boundary around the agreed meeting time, and my being on time in the meeting of my commitment to myself? As long as I believe that my statement "you're always late" is about the other, then I am waiting for the other to change and to take responsibility for the unwitting 'neglect' that I am perpetrating on myself by waiting beyond the agreed time. There is some hidden insecurity that leads me to do that, and unless this becomes conscious I will cleverly hold with the illusion that when I talk I am talking about the other person.

Perhaps 'being the nice, patient person' is my psychological safeguarding means of getting recognition and I do not want to jeopardise that protection by taking action for myself by going about my business when the other person fails to arrive at the agreed time. Another possibility is that at a core level I dread conflict and any confrontation means risking it and so I avoid it. Until I find the psychosocial safety to begin to resolve my current wise dependence on 'being the nice, patient person' to gain recognition and to begin to stand firm in the face of conflict, I will not allow consciousness of what I say as being about myself to emerge.

The other wonderful creative illusion among many of us adults is that what another says is about us. This is the situation when you personalise what another says rather than seeing that what the other says is of, about and belongs with the other. When you personalise, for example, what you perceive as a judgment – "you're so selfish" – there is a protective purpose, unconsciously created, to internalising the message that belongs to the other. Possible psychologically safeguarding protective intentions may be not wanting others to see how badly you see yourself, or fear of conflict, or not wanting to reveal inner doubts about your worth and intelligence.

Common protective responses to the verbal expression of another are internal blaming of Self, or silent emotional or physical withdrawal, or taking on responsibility for what the other person says by attempting to appease or to keep hidden the truths that dare not be expressed. How adults then respond to another's protective communication always reveals where they are within themselves – either separate from the person communicating or enmeshed. Examples of unconscious protective communication are:

- Being judgmental
- Being dominant
- Being controlling
- Being passive
- Being arrogant
- Being manipulative
- Being verbally threatening
- Being blaming of Self or others
- Being rigid
- Not listening
- Being hypercritical
- Being emotionless

As already indicated, each of these ways of communicating ingeniously hides an aspect of oneself that to date dared not be revealed, due to threats experienced as children and continuing as adults. Possible hidden issues include:

- Being real
- Being authentic

- Being spontaneous
- Being different
- Being assertive
- Being one's own individual Self
- Being expressive of one's truth
- Being vocal about violations – emotional, sexual, physical or intellectual
- Being fearless
- Being emotionally expressive

Resolution of protective communication involves finding psychological safety to get behind the amazingly built protective walls and bring out what lies hidden. When adults, particularly those in leadership and management roles, communicate protectively, then issues that need resolution go underground and fester. The sad fact is that if leading players in our holding worlds do not encounter the psychological safety to take responsibility and seek psychological support for the resolution of hidden unconscious issues, the outlook is not good for anyone in those holding worlds.

What arises in adults is about the adults!

An unspoken secret is that 'what arises in me is about me', and any attempt to voice that truth can be responded to with hostility. Of course, such hostility is a revelation of the inner world of the person being hostile – a reality that could be dangerous to voice for the person being authentic.

What is it that makes it so difficult as an adult to own what arises in me as being about me – be it a dream, feeling, thought, image, action, word, or illness? The answer to that question lies in the answer to another question: has my life to date been a series of safe moments with a few dangerous ones or a series of dangerous moments with a few safe ones? If the latter is the case, it is more likely that owning and being responsible for what arises in me could prove highly threatening.

When I own what arises in me, I will speak and act from an 'I' place, a place of conscious psychological safety and self-realisation. When I disown what arises, I tend to unconsciously protectively speak from a 'you' or 'they' place and blame others, the system, the world or God for how my life is. There is great wisdom – though not consciousness – in such projections. The wisdom is that I shine the spotlight of blame and responsibility on others, thereby cleverly exonerating myself from being criticised and judged. Resolution of these projections can be effected only by finding psychological safety to hold and value everything that arises as being about Self.

In times of economic depression, social disharmony or political repression, unless financial, social, educational and political leaders come to conscious psychological safety responsibility for their practices, it is unlikely that anything will be learned from economic crises. Experience has shown, time after time, that we do not learn from history unless adults find psychological safety to own mistakes, fears, insecurities, aggression, greed, passivity and rigidities. This may seem a bridge too far but this is a bridge that each of us needs to cross – and actually wants to cross – but only when there is psychological safety to do so. It is in each person finding psychological safety and slowly coming to consciousness that real progress can be made within society.

It is individuals who make decisions – not systems – and it is only individuals who can choose to make different decisions. There is no such thing as a fearless organisation or a fearful organisation! Organisations have no head or heart but individuals do. In becoming conscious of the foregoing, it becomes possible for each of us as adults to affect the world at large by bringing conscious heart and head to the people with whom we interact and to the health, social, educational, religious, work and political systems in which we live. This is a major challenge to take on, and the question arises how this conscious process might be encouraged and supported.

The future of society never lies with children – it is always with adults. It is adults who need to find the psychological safety and support to reflect on how each relates to Self, to others and to the world. We, as adults, continually spill the beans on our interior worlds with every thought, word, feeling and action. When we begin the process of holding each manifestation of our interiority and examining what it reveals about the relationship with Self and others and what new choices and actions are being called for, then progress towards consciousness, self-realisation and open care for Self and owning our own words and actions will gradually emerge. Such reflection and contemplation will result in radically different ways of being in the world, a radicalism that is sorely needed in today's world.

Owning what arises in us as adults is not optional, rather it is an urgent aspiration that in truth all adults secretly hold. It is critical that leaders, in particular parents, teachers, politicians, clergy, health and welfare services providers, business managers, be provided with the psychological safety opportunities to examine their lives, so that they can take up the challenge of knowing Self, and can create the emotional, social and intellectual safety for children – and other adults – to retain the untethered expression of radiant mind with which we all so powerfully and eagerly start out in life.

Children's psychological safeguarding

Oscar Wilde made the famous comment that "youth is wasted on the young". With hindsight that can seem to be the case but children, like adults, are where they need to be and can act only from that place. When parents and teachers find the inner psychological safety to stand in their own shoes, they truly appreciate and understand the myriad of challenges that face young people, threats that add to those they are already experiencing and that they dare not have the inner solidity to express. When this is the case, then all sorts of unconscious psychological safeguarding strategies are employed by the young person to wisely avoid the challenge of becoming independent.

It is frequently the case that parents and teachers experience considerable frustration with young people who are not committed to their studies. Common complaints are that these students are 'wasters', 'lazy', 'hyperactive', 'bored', 'timid', 'absent', 'irresponsible', 'not doing their homework', 'distracted', 'ungrateful', 'difficult', 'aggressive'. In spite of the common perception that these students are 'troublesome', the reality is that students are not out to make life difficult for teachers or parents, but they are out to show how difficult life is for them. But because it is psychologically unsafe to speak the truth of what is happening in their relationships with parents and teachers, students unconsciously and creatively find hidden – as opposed to real and authentic – ways of expressing their inner turmoil. The hope is that some adult will spot the deeper meaning of their 'difficult' behaviours and offer the love, support and belief in them for them to communicate their distress.

There is nearly always a double meaning to words and actions. When teachers and parents react to students' troubling behaviours, the basis of their response is a literal interpretation of the specific difficult response of the student. Of course, when teachers react to students' behaviours, the teachers themselves are not trying to make life difficult for students, but they too are attempting to show how difficult life is for them. There is some chance that a student's distress will be spotted by an adult who is in a psychological safety place to understand the hidden messages, but who helps and supports teachers?

A literal interpretation of the above listed complaints of parents and teachers means that students will be blamed, considered irresponsible and deserving of a 'good telling off'. Such threatening responses will only exacerbate the students' inner turmoil and there will be an escalation of the difficult responses.

When the ingenious, symbolic and metaphorical meanings and deeper intention of the distressing behaviours are sought, an entirely different response emerges. It is crucial to recognise that the deeper meanings of students' challenging responses are particular to each student and it is only by talking with the student and exploring the hidden intentions that the true meaning emerges. When considering typical complaints, described below, of the parents and teachers of young people, the interpretations provided are possibilities of what may be troubling the adult in the situation — not the young person! Only the students themselves can reveal what is going on for them.

Generally speaking, the student's unconscious psychological safeguarding behaviours are masking issues about how he or she is seen in the family, particularly by each parent, and by teachers and by Self. When a teacher unconsciously repeats the painful experiences that students have already encountered and continue to endure in their homes, the students will wisely perceive the teacher as threatening as he or she does in response to the unconscious abandonment behaviours of one or other or both parents. Clearly, when this happens, the inner turmoil of the young person is compounded.

Typical Complaints by Parents/Teachers about Young People's Behaviour	Possible Symbolic Meaning for Parent/Teacher
• 'Waster'	• 'In what way am I "wasting" valuable time in care of myself?'
• 'No homework'	• 'What inner homework do I need to do to be at home with myself?'
• 'Lazy'	• 'No energy for myself'
• 'Difficult'	• 'There are difficult issues with myself that are calling for my attention'
• 'Hyperactive'	• 'Too much going on with myself; no peace in myself'
• 'Distracted'	• 'Personal life off-track; not attracted to myself'
• 'Bored'	• 'What was bored into me about my worth has hurt me deeply'; 'I have no interest in myself'
• 'Tired'	• No longer energised by what I do'; 'I'm tired of myself'

• 'Irresponsible'	• 'I'm being unconsciously reactive rather than consciously proactive'; 'I unconsciously struggle with taking conscious responsibility for myself'
• 'Absent'	• 'I'm not present to the young person'; 'I'm not present to myself'
• 'Aggressive'	• 'I'm hostile towards myself'; 'I hate myself'
• 'In another world'	• 'The real world is too painful a place to be'; 'I have no sense of an inner world'
• 'Failing'	• 'There have been many affective failures in my story to date'; 'I see myself as a failure'
• 'Ungrateful'	• 'I have never felt appreciated at home or at school'; 'I have no appreciation of myself'

Creating psychological safety for parents and teachers to realise that anything they say about a young person or, indeed, any psychiatric label that is attached to a young person, is 100% about the parent or teacher (or the professional person) who assesses and labels the young person. This is not a criticism of these adults; on the contrary, it is a matter of concern and a realisation that adults need to be attended to first. When adults are in a conscious psychological safety inner place, they automatically own their own responses as being about themselves and their response to the young person who is troubled or troubling will be one of gentle enquiry and with a knowing that the young person is the expert on his or her life. It is a common experience for many young people who are suffering that no such enquiry is made about their story to date – most particularly, on their key relationships – with each parent, grandparents, siblings, teachers and peers. My own experience is that a thorough exploration of both the outer and inner worlds of young people brings to light the origins of and the ingenious creative and heroic safeguarding purposes of what adults perceive as their difficult behaviours.

Considerable patience is essential when helping students to reveal and resolve their troubled worlds. Teachers require the cooperation of parents and when this is not forthcoming, then teachers, from their own inner domain of psychological safety, can offer the student unconditional regard, understanding, compassion and support. When a student is a young adult, the teacher can champion the student to stand for Self and live his or her own life and not the life of parents. Difficult emotional territory for teachers and students to trek, but then teaching without conscious affect is not teaching at all. Availing of the services of a co-creational relationship practitioner or counsellor or psychotherapist may well be needed for both the student who is troubled, his or her peers, and for the parent and teacher who is carrying so many responsibilities as well as their own unresolved abandonments when they were children.

.

Chapter Four:
Psychological Safety in Homes and Schools

- Psychological Safety and Emergence of Realisations
- There is Homework and Homework – Psychological Safety Parenting
- There is Classwork and Classwork – Psychological Safety Teaching
- Attending to the Inner Course of Learning – Psychological Safety Living

Psychological safety and emergence of realisations

The ingenuity that creates the unconscious world is the same ingenuity that creates the conscious world. The origins of the unconscious world are all the psychological safeguarding responses that parents, teachers and other significant adults bring to their relationships with children. These threatening responses are part and parcel of the unconscious genius worlds of these adults. Protectiveness then begets protectiveness and, of course, openness begets openness. The transition from unconscious living to conscious living occurs when psychological safety – emotional, social, intellectual, physical, sexual and creative – is present, this being as true for adults as it is for children.

Many realisations emerge when such profound psychological safeties are present. It is useful to chart the principal realisations that can emerge and that wisely support the shift from unconsciousness to consciousness, hiding to emerging, from depression to expression, from fearfulness to fearlessness and from dependence to independence.

Realisations – When psychological safety is present

1. Parents' own conscious psychological safety
2. Relationship with Self – the fundamental realisation
3. Teachers' own conscious psychological safety relationship with Self – an equally fundamental realisation
4. Prioritising children's wellbeing – only possible when 1 and 2 are present
5. The meaning of unconsciousness – hidden world
6. The meaning of consciousness – open world
7. Psychological safety relationship lies at the heart of affective and effective parenting
8. Psychological safety relationship lies at the heart of affective and effective teaching
9. Conscious psychological safety parenting
10. Conscious psychological safety teaching
11. Conscious psychological safety learning

12. Each parent has his or her own unique story
13. Each teacher has his or her own unique story
14. Each child has his or her own unique story
15. Parents are not out to make life difficult for children
16. Children are not out to make life difficult for parents
17. Students are not out to make life difficult for teachers
18. Teachers are not out to make life difficult for students
19. Teaching and learning are separate issues
20. The adventure of learning
21. Intelligence and knowledge are separate issues
22. The unconscious blocks to affective and effective teaching and learning
23. Achievement as metaphor
24. Parents' fearful responses as metaphors
25. Teachers' fearful responses as metaphors
26. Children's fearful responses as metaphors
27. The creativity of conflict
28. Psychological safety or safeguarding is always present!

(All of the above are discussed throughout the book and can be accessed through the index for page numbers).

It is evident from the foregoing how minimal is the realisation, the consciousness, that all our fearful responses are a continuing loudspeaker of all that we fear and have repressed. Our unconsciously designed psychological safeguarding also points to early threatening environments of invasive parental behaviours, hostile school environments and, sometimes, difficult socioeconomic pressures, political and global threats. Nevertheless, the major sources are within homes, schools and communities, but all fearful responses, amazingly created, both by adults and by children, are the doorway to consciousness of our fullness, individuality, unconditional lovability, and being consciously free.

Picture again the radiant mind and behaviours of the toddler – creativity, excitement, eagerness to learn, spontaneity, fearlessness, emotional expressiveness and receptivity, awe, persistence, not being fazed by mistakes or failures, energetic. How many of these aspects of your true nature are buried and awaiting resurrection? You have seen that when psychological safety is present, slowly but surely reawakenings occur. Finding such psychological safety in a world of people dominated by unconscious fear is difficult; hence the continuing seeking out of psychotherapeutic and psychoanalytic practitioners, relationship mentors and business coaches. In these professionals continuing to deepen psychological safety to examine their own screen worlds, the depth and breadth of that examination is what determines the level of psychological safety they will bring to the individuals, couples, families and workplace personnel who seek out their professional practice.

It can be seen from the paucity of realisations how the unconditional relationship with Self and others lies at the heart of conscious open contact – especially between parent and child, teacher and student, husband and wife, manager and employee. The bottom line is that any adult, irrespective of gender, age, status, education or wealth, can see in the other only what he or she sees in Self. Recall that where adults are is where they need to be, and that nobody deliberately wants to make life difficult for others, but instead are screaming out how difficult life is for them. Unless their torment is recognised, held compassionately and patiently, then that torment will cascade down through the generations. The German poet Rilke put it well when he wrote: "Everything terrible is something crying out for love."

When adults emerge into consciousness, they redeem and begin to express fearlessly the amazing qualities of their true nature:

- Individuality
- Ingenuity
- Difference
- Eagerness to learn
- Unconditional love
- Risk-taking, experimentation
- Humour
- Emotional expressiveness and receptivity
- Spontaneity
- Kindness
- Boundaries
- Fearlessness
- Openness
- Separateness
- Conscious ownership of one's own life
- Empowerment
- Creativity
- Embracement of failure as opportunity
- Non-judgment
- No confusion of Self with success
- Spirituality
- Fairness
- Communication from the inside-out

- Imagination
- Understanding
- Proactions

Considerable psychological safety to engage in this conscious work is required for all of the above qualities to become part of adults' daily behavioural repertoire. Further elucidation of that inner journey follows under the headings:

- There is homework and homework – conscious psychological safety parenting
- There is classwork and classwork – conscious psychological safety teaching
- Attending to the inner course of learning – conscious psychological safety living

There is homework and homework – psychological safety parenting

A mother contacted me once regarding her difficulties with her 14-year-old son when it came to getting him to do his homework. Over several years he had thrown temper tantrums and showed great defiance to her attempts to make him do his homework. She had been prompted to make contact with me because his defiance had escalated to the extent of lashing out physically at her. Research shows that many mothers do experience considerable rebellious behaviours from teenage sons and require guidance and support to maintain definite boundaries around their own physical and emotional wellbeing. Maintenance of boundaries creates a psychological safety for the emergence of whatever is troubling the young person. When a child has been turned off learning there is always some hidden emotional turmoil behind the challenging behaviours being exhibited.

There is no doubt that parents want to ensure that their children fulfil the responsibilities of being a student and part of those responsibilities is completing their homework in the required way. But the way a parent approaches a child on the issue needs serious consideration because, ironically, parents themselves also may, unwittingly, not be fulfilling their responsibilities of 'homework' which, sometimes, can underlie the student's reluctance towards or hatred of doing school homework.

A word of caution here: a child's difficulties with homework may have several sources, not just home-based ones. Frequently, adults relay stories of humiliation and ridicule in classrooms. If it is the presence of psychological safety in parents that leads them to doing their homework in terms of creating quality relationships, it is also the psychological safety in each teacher that enables the creation of a homely and safe atmosphere within classrooms – this is the teacher's homework. The more adults find the psychological safety to consciously take on their responsibilities, the more children follow suit.

It is well known that each classroom is a different culture and the architect of the classroom culture is principally the teacher. The teacher does need the back-up support of the board of management, school principal and colleagues. When such support is not available or is weak, there is an urgent cry for the reasons for this lack of 'homework' to be addressed. It is the case that when we are unwittingly fearful that it is the sty in the other's eye we see and not the sty in our own eye. Eye in this context symbolically represents the 'I', the Self, and the sty metaphorically represents the blocks that are there to being fully Self-expressive.

Back to the story of the 14-year-old's revelation to me that he hated school, hated homework, and could not wait to leave school. When he was four years of age he had engaged in an exploration of his father's office, only to be physically beaten and harshly corrected for making a mess. The conscious parent knows that making a mess is central to children's quest to make sense of and to understand the complex worlds within which they live. Patience, understanding and enquiry by the father into the child's explorations would have won the child's heart and helped him retain his natural curiosity, love and eagerness to learn. What followed for this child was a clever repression of those core qualities with the resultant protective hate of learning and homework.

It is the wonderful nature of children to be curious, adventurous, dare-devil and eager to learn. When these core qualities have gone missing, something has happened in the relationship between the child and some significant adult − parent, teacher, grandparent, child-minder. Unless the rift in the relationship is resolved, the child may not recover the core qualities that have had to be repressed. Why would the child risk harsh abandonment again? Only when the child feels again the psychological safety to express is the child likely to begin to take the risk again to learn and explore. Interestingly, with the 14-year-old in the present example, there was one teacher for whom he was motivated to work and, significantly, this was a teacher who befriended him.

Both psychological safety parents and teachers realise that the sine qua non for a child's love of learning to thrive is an unconditionally loving relationship and expression of belief in the child's genius. When academic performance or the doing of homework become more important than their unique presence, children will either rebel against learning or become addicted to proving themselves through it − which is even more problematic than the rebellion. In either case, fear dogs the child's steps.

Patience, good humour, expressions of encouragement, support and understanding are essential psychological safety aspects of helping children with homework. These qualities are also required in parents for them to do their homework. Certainly, the absence of annoyance, criticism, comparisons, irritability, advice-giving, cynicism, sarcasm and impatience is central to creating a psychological safety relationship for children to enjoy and be challenged by study. Children's motivation to learn is seriously threatened when adults verbally or non-verbally or physically hurt or threaten them. As George Bernard Shaw said "You cannot cure children's problems by hurting them." What Shaw did not see was that unresolved hurts in adults need attending to before they can attend to young people's hidden hurts and fearful responses.

There is classwork and classwork – psychological safety teaching

Conscious responsibility emerges when a teacher recognises that no matter what response arises in one, that response is about one's own interior world and is not caused by the students' (or other people's) behaviours. In many ways, this reality provides great hope, because it is not within one's power to resolve the challenging responses of another, whether student or colleague or parent, but each of us does have all the resources to understand and take charge of our own protective responses. Helping the student is a separate issue to resolving any annoyance arising in the teacher and entails creating a psychological safety and supportive relationship for the student to examine his or her own troubling responses and to discover what is the psychological safety they require to gradually come out from their architecturally designed protective walls.

Some common experiences among teachers are stress, loss of control, irritability, frustration, exhaustion, loss of motivation, illness, absenteeism and burn-out. Each of these experiences is an opportunity for the teacher to come into deeper knowing of Self and a more enduring conscious Self-reliance. The inner sources of teachers' challenging behaviours towards students are particular to each individual teacher; there are no common causes or solutions. For example, one teacher's growing sense of frustration with his work may be due to an underlying fear of authority and a wise deficit in authoritativeness within Self; whereas for another it may be an underlying need to be liked by students and an inner alienation from Self.

In the first instance, the teacher looks to authority figures, rather than to Self, for approval and direction. In other words, what he wants from his school principal is what he needs to give himself, but is in too much fear to assert his own worth in the face of the principal and the first authority figures – one or both of his parents or teachers. What he now requires is the psychological safety and support to develop an authorship of Self – the true meaning of the word authority. When this is not forthcoming, the teacher may need to seek psychotherapy or relationship mentoring which will offer that much-needed psychological safety.

In the second example above, the teacher who wants to be liked by her students is creatively making her students the substitute source for what she needs to do for herself – love and appreciate Self. Again, the source is in childhood and not having experienced being liked and loved by one or both parents. It is highly emotionally threatening for the teacher to assert her likeability and lovability as she dreads re-experiencing the darkness of rejection. By bending over backwards for students, and feeling frustrated that no matter how hard she tries, some students still express hostility, she feels threatened and teaching becomes a difficult experience. What she is looking for from students is what she is secretly longing to give to herself. When she does that, she will perceive students' hostile responses as being about themselves and, whilst retaining clear and definite boundaries around respect for herself, she will offer students the psychological safety to examine and resolve the source of their challenging behaviours. She will not abandon herself in her offering of support to students.

When considering these common experiences of teachers, possible unconscious and conscious metaphorical interpretations are as follows:

Stress: Metaphorically represents *emphasis* and what the teacher is presently fearful of seeing:

- Pressure and strain to prove Self (protective behaviours; unconscious psychological safeguarding genius)
- Hidden issue: need to consciously approve of Self (conscious psychological safety response being called out for)

Loss of Control: Symbolically represents a fear of possessing an inner stronghold of Self:

- Pressure to control students (protective: unconscious psychological safeguarding genius)
- Hidden issue: to take conscious control of Self (conscious psychological safety being called out for)

Irritability: Metaphorically represents being at odds with Self:

- Annoyed that students are not conforming (protective: unconscious psychological safeguarding genius)
- Hidden issue: to separate behaviour from person (conscious psychological safety being called out for)

Exhaustion: Symbolically – no energy for Self:

- An unconscious avoidance strategy – how can I be expected to work when exhausted? (protective: unconscious psychological safeguarding genius)

- Hidden issue: to become energised whereby work becomes love made visible (conscious psychological safety being called out for)

Loss of Motivation: Symbolically – no inner movement:

- Looking to others to provide motivation (protective: unconscious psychological safeguarding genius)
- Hidden issue: to *move* in the direction of a deep regard for Self and a resurrection of natural curiosity (conscious psychological safety being called out for)

Illness: Symbolically – an inner dis-ease that needs attending to:

- Unconsciously provides a way out from the threat of teaching (unconscious psychological safeguarding genius)
- Hidden issue: to discover the inner wellness of the Self (conscious psychological safety being called out for)

Absenteeism: Metaphorically – being absent from Self:

- When I'm not at school, then I cannot fail or be criticised (protective: unconscious psychological safeguarding genius)
- Hidden issue: to become present to one's Ingenious and Sacred Self (conscious psychological safety being called out for)

Burn-out: Symbolically – the fire within me is extinguished:

- Conveys "don't expect any more of me" (protective: unconscious psychological safeguarding genius)

- Hidden issue: to reignite the fire of love and belief in Self and learning (conscious psychological safety being called out for)

Whether it is teachers or students, when they live out their lives from the place of fearfulness rather than fearlessness, inevitably challenging responses that threaten the wellbeing of others will be unconsciously created. But it is only when the protective responses to being fearless, real and authentic are dissolved that the threats to the wellbeing of others disappear. It is an unconscious genius reality that teachers who are passive, perfectionist and overdemanding of themselves unwittingly pose threats to the wellbeing of students, as do those teachers who are aggressive, cross, irritable, cynical and sarcastic. The more frequent, intense and enduring are teachers acting in or acting out unconscious behaviours, the more they are creatively stuck in an interior darkness and the greater the threat to the wellbeing of students. A school culture that provides psychological safety opportunities for continuing personal reflection among teachers goes a long way to ensuring conscious teaching.

Attending to the inner course of learning – psychological safety living

One of the most important developments over recent decades has been the opportunity for life-long adult education. But one of my concerns is that education has been more geared towards career development or having something to do during the dark winter evenings rather than the pursuit of personal consciousness. All education – no matter the subject area – needs to address the in-formation of students and not just provide information. Education is no index of consciousness and that has been so evident in what seems like the endless repetition of the crises in the social, health, religious, economic and political arenas across the globe. Bullying, too, has emerged as a frequent experience in many workplaces and that includes universities.

Similarly, the aggressive behaviour of our political leaders leaves a lot to be understood and one needs to ask the question: what educational process has led these elected individuals to behave in ways that any teacher in a primary or second-level classroom would challenge firmly? It appears to be that whilst the educational opportunities that are widely available are to be lauded, the intentions underlying these courses require examination. When delivering a course, a psychological safety teacher or lecturer will first consider their own interiority, and what their teaching reflects of their own beliefs, understanding of Self and how they want to be in this world.

Conscious teachers are particularly focused on the inner course of students because they know that their responses to what is being taught will be totally determined by the present state of their inner terrain and level of personal psychological safety and consciousness. It is by encouraging and noticing students' responses to the material that teachers gain insight into the students' inner worlds and into the unconscious psychological safeguarding processes that are guiding their responses, and then together what they gain from the particular course they are attending can be maximised. Whether or not lecturers see it, each of their students has a different teacher and each student responds to what the lecturer says in a different way – no matter what the subject. Psychological safety education is geared to the individual and it is the conscious teacher that knows that you cannot address a group; a group has no heart or head.

There is an old saying 'when the student is ready, the teacher appears' which suggests that some students are not ready for learning or, indeed, that some teachers are not ready to teach. I believe that the student is always ready to learn but it may not be the knowledge being presented by the teacher. For example, a colleague of mine suggested that you cannot teach a hungry child!

My response was that the child is ready to speak about his hunger and the teacher's focus needs to be where the child's attention is.

Similarly, when a student in a classroom is experiencing inner turmoil, it is the conscious teacher who notices and provides the opportunity on a one-to-one basis for the student to speak about what he or she needs to resolve the blocks to psychological safety living. To condemn the student's inattention out of hand is a call for the teacher to examine his or her own inner terrain and ask the question: "How is it that I'm not in a place to draw out and create the psychological safety for this student to acquire the consciousness he or she needs to resolve his or her inner turmoil?" After all, the word education comes from the Latin word *educare*, meaning to draw out.

Education is not about instilling information but about creating the opportunity for the student and teacher to know Self and the world. On this latter point, a teacher's level of psychological safety or psychological safeguarding plays an essential role in how he or she teaches. After all, personal affectiveness and effectiveness is the basis of professional effectiveness but, regrettably, the practice of examining one's inner and outer behaviour in order to resolve workplace issues – emotional, social, physical, intellectual, sexual and behavioural – that all adults, undoubtedly, carry from childhood has not been an integral part of the training of educational and other professionals. Society pays dearly for this serious, albeit unconscious, omission.

Research now shows that it is deep unconscious emotional processes – and not intelligence – that determines not only *what* we learn but *how* we learn. Equally, such unconscious processes determine *what* and *how* teachers teach. Opportunities, too, need to be created for third-level students to ask the question: "What attracts me to a particular course?"

- Is it to please my parents or others?
- Is it to impress others?
- Is it to fill a void?
- Is it because I couldn't think what else to do?
- Is it because the subject energises me?
- Is it because it is something I have always wanted to do?

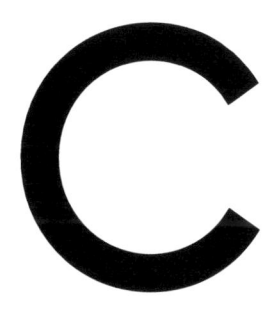

Chapter Five:
Parents' Psychological Safety First

- Parents' Psychological Safety First
- Parents' Psychological Safeguarding
- Parents' Psychological Safety

Parents' psychological safety first

Some years ago, I presented a talk at a mental health conference which I had titled 'Parents First'. The previous two speakers spoke about the parents of children who require intensive psychiatric care – often residential care – as having mental illnesses for which there was no cure! I was quite shocked by the psychiatric labelling of parents in deep distress and by the hopelessness of the health professionals themselves and the communication of that pessimism to the parents and to their troubled and troubling children. The hypothesis of mental illness is often put forward as if there were no doubt about it, whereas the reality is that there is a large body of research (Davies 2013, Carlat 2010, Bentall 2004, James 2016) which contradicts this hypothesis and shows no substantial evidence to support it. Certainly, these parents' protective safeguarding responses − chronic anxiety, depression, paranoia, substance addictions, hallucinations and delusions − are 'dis-eases', communicating inner terror or fear, repressions and multiple unresolved traumas. It is tragic that the very people they seek help from abandon them and, unwittingly, re-traumatise them.

At the conference when I stood up to speak, I expressed my distress at what I had heard and said I would like to present my understanding of the parents' − and, indeed, of the children's − manifestations of their deep inner turmoil. I told the audience that when I completed my PhD in Clinical Psychology, which was primarily cognitive-behavioural in its approach, I believed that individuals who experienced psychoses were mentally ill and that those who presented with neuroses were conditioned. In terms of those who were given the 'psychotic' and the 'bi-polar depression' labels, I saw them as needing psychiatric intervention: hospitalisation, medication, even regrettably electro-convulsive shock therapy. As far as the neuroses went, I believed that individuals so labelled could be deconditioned and reconditioned.

I began my work in state psychiatric hospitals, first in England and subsequently in Ireland. When I went down into the back-wards and encountered individuals who had been incarcerated for years in these dungeons and heavily medicated, and often having received multiple electro-shock treatments, I was shocked to discover that their diagnosis took no account of their often horrific stories. When I created relationships with some of these individuals the wisdom and creativity of their so-called insane responses began to make total sense to me. It was quite a cataclysmic experience for me as it became apparent to me that 'madness' did not exist but 'maddening' experiences do occur and it is these that need to be the focus of our attention. Human suffering is a path, not a pathology, and the path is to discover what lies hidden.

Similarly, my clinical psychology training fell apart for me with the realisation that individuals are not conditioned but devise the most amazing – unconsciously – psychological safeguarding strategies to survive the adverse experiences they encountered when children and continued to experience as adults. When I responded to these individuals seeking my help with an attitude of "that behaviour is maladaptive or dysfunctional" and "your thoughts are irrational", it gradually dawned on me that those behaviours and cognitions I was being critical of were powerful means of reducing threats and highly creative and functional. In examining my own protectors in therapy and in seeing the amazing survival strategies of those I labelled 'psychotic' or 'neurotic', all that I had learned at university over eight years collapsed for me and a whole new understanding of psychosocial, and also physical suffering, slowly but surely began to emerge for me. At the conference I spoke about my work with individuals over the years. I expressed my belief that story is a powerful means of communicating the nature of human suffering as story touches all our lives in one way or another.

One case I presented was what I had named the 'cake story'. This was a situation where a five-year-old had been put into foster care due to her biological single-parent mother having addictions to alcohol and drugs, resulting in harsh neglect of the child's overall wellbeing. She was allowed supervised access to her child. On her child's sixth birthday she accompanied a child-care worker to attend her child's celebration in her foster home. She arrived with a birthday cake, beautifully iced with figurines and six candles. The child was thrilled and when it came time to cut the cake, she excitedly blew out the candles and with her mother's help cut the cake. The cake burst open, filled with cigarette butts, faeces and other rubbish. Her mother turned to her and screamed "This is how I see you, you little bitch."

The child felt annihilated and the care worker quickly removed the mother from her child's precious presence. All present condemned the mother as 'bad, bad, bad', but nobody saw that the mother protectively saw herself as 'rubbish' and unconsciously had projected that on to her child. Of course, the child creatively personalised what the mother had said; children depend on parents to mirror, affirm, and be in awe of their unique and unrepeatable presence. It was wise for the child to personalise because she certainly now will not put herself out there again for such devastating rejection; she will retreat, withdraw, become passive or appeasing but she will not risk reaching out again.

John Welwood (2005) captures this sad phenomenon when he writes:

> "Unfortunately, most parents cannot help their children recognise or honour their deeper potentials. They see children through a glass darkly because that is how they see themselves. No matter how much our parents love us, they generally see their version of who we are, as reflected in the dark glass of their hopes, fears, expectations and unmet needs.
>
> "This is not something to blame them for… they simply couldn't give their children a kind of recognition they never got nor gave themselves. Nor could they allow their children to have feelings, needs or sensitivities they were never allowed to have themselves. The child is like an open hand that gradually starts to contract and close."

In the above 'cake story' the person who was seriously crying out for help was the mother – parents first! But nobody recognised that the mother's 'rubbishing' of her child was echoing how she had been rubbished as a child herself by her parents. In relegating this mother's devastating behaviour to the realm of mental illness and incurable addictions, she once more experiences the savage abandonment she encountered in her childhood. Inevitably, her child is smartly going to create her psychological safeguarding responses and the more traumatic the abandonment, the greater the protectors created. What is likely to happen is that the child's means of unconsciously safeguarding herself and trying to draw attention to her overwhelming emotional pain will be labelled and even medicated, thereby repeating the endless cycle of suffering.

Once the child is viewed as troubled and troubling, rather than unconsciously resourceful and attempting to alert others to the stark pain of rejection by her mother and abandonment by her father, then her necessarily having to feel nothing for herself – not unlike her mother – does not get resolved. The necessity for healthcare professionals to realise the unconscious psychological safeguarding nature of human suffering in their practice is an urgent issue required for the benefit of all concerned. It is not unusual that the healthcare professional may be more in need of psychological safety and understanding than the individuals he or she may be attempting to help – in this case, care professionals first!

From the teacher's point of view, the child who presents with either acting out or acting in her hidden traumas and abandonment from key figures in her life, the need to involve the parents or foster parents becomes paramount. There is no doubt that the teacher's unconditional holding and understanding of the child will make a significant difference to the child; the contrary is also true. But, of course, the teacher will have a minimum of 20-25 other children to relate to and to teach, and it is important that the school employs relationship mentors or psychotherapists who have an in-depth co-creational understanding of protective behaviours and know how to create psychological safety with the child, the parents, the class teacher and the school principal that will seek to bring to consciousness what has lain hidden for each of them.

It is unrealistic to expect teachers to be mentors, and because they have not had the opportunity to re-examine their own lives, not infrequently the 'difficult' behaviours of parents and their children can trigger protective responses on their part. Somehow schools – government policies – have not focused on the total development of the child and nothing is more important than the emotional and social wellbeing of children. When emotional and social wellbeing are present, all else follows. Government policy needs to recognise that parenting and, indeed, teaching, are rocket science and that continual personal reflection courses for all prospective parents and teachers are very much needed. Ongoing parenting courses and accessible support are critical for the total wellbeing of parents and their children. Every human being suffers to some extent – a sizeable number suffer to a great extent – and the resolution of suffering creates a society where our power beyond measure is consciously employed for the benefit of all.

Parents' psychological safeguarding

Curiously, a common illusion is that we all come from happy families. Over the years, many individuals during their initial contact rush to assure me that they had come from the 'perfect' family, were loved by both parents and, accordingly, there is no need to go back to the past looking for the source of their depression or chronic anxiety or extreme stress or paranoia. There is genius and great wisdom in this illusion as it ensures that the parents will be left in their safeguarded place of being 'perfect' and, most potently, for their offspring it serves to psychologically shield them from any further experiences of parental abandonment. There is an old saying that captures this process: 'once bitten, twice shy'; this saying was reinforced for me by an adolescent who when asked "How many times have you been bitten?" replied spontaneously "Eight hundred times." Eight hundred times bitten, ten thousand times shy of risking any further rejection! Of course, as the individual rests into the comfort of being unconditionally loved and held without judgment, gradually, at his or her own pace, he or she reveals the full story of life to date.

One of the privileged experiences I have had over the years is when a mother declared "I don't love my children." I felt privileged because I wonder to whom else would that mother have revealed this painful reality; the possibility of harsh judgment would be high. This particular story will confirm the prime intention of this chapter which is to emphasise Parents' Psychological Safety First.

When the mother made the above declaration, I acknowledged what she had said and how special I felt in her choosing to tell me. I then gently asked her "How do you feel about yourself?" Her immediate answer was "I hate myself." I followed this reply by saying "I am so impressed that you have found a way to unwittingly express your inner turmoil by projecting it on to your children. Furthermore, you not loving your children shows me that you were not loved as a child, and until you come into that place of loving yourself – being mother, father, friend, lover, partner to yourself – you will wisely retain your belief that you do not love your children. But I can assure you that when love awakens in your heart for yourself, it will also awaken for your children."

Interestingly, I subsequently met with one of her sons, aged around eight years at the time, for a session during which I was very moved by the child and told him so and let him know that I would miss him. For months afterwards he kept saying to his mother "Tony said he would miss me." The hidden message here could have been "Mum, Tony misses me, but do you ever miss me?" or "Mum, you miss seeing me all the time." It takes the world to raise a child and it is important for each of us as adults – therapists, teachers, social workers, psychologists, school principals, neighbours and so on – to realise that our contact can be a lifeline for a child who feels unloved and unwanted.

At one point, the mother rang me anxiously relaying that the boy had developed an obsessive-compulsive disorder. The child was convinced that all adults had germs and if he went near them or even sat on a chair they had occupied that he would be infected. Furthermore, he now believed that adults smell and he needed to stay a long way away from them. When he came to see me, we connected quite quickly. When I enquired how he was feeling, his reply was "Very sad." He told me that his Dad – mother and father had separated – kept promising to take him places but time and time again he would fail to turn up. I acknowledged the boy's sadness and followed with "And I believe you are convinced adults have germs." He nodded his head to his fear of infection and gave a definite nod to "and adults smell too." When I asked how he felt adults had been with him he replied "They have hurt me." My response was "Aren't you the clever boy to find ways of steering clear of adults so that you don't get hurt?"

Subsequent to my time with him, and with his permission, I relayed to his parents the sources of his creative obsessional behaviour and showed how it was in their hands to resolve the child's hurts. The father did make a greater effort and mother continued her own therapy. She came to the place where she could hug and kiss him and, at one point, when she asked the child "How do you feel when I hug you?" the child heartbreakingly replied "I don't feel you hate me anymore." Trust, of necessity, is built slowly. Two years later the child indicated that he truly felt loved and expressed high praise for his mother's work on herself. In terms of school work, his attainments accelerated and learning re-emerged as an exciting experience. Teachers were asking the question "What has changed?" The short answer was "Love is present."

Parents have so many responsibilities in terms of the physical, emotional, social, sexual, intellectual, behavioural, creative and spiritual development of their children. They are the primary educators and it is well established by research that the pre-school years of a child's life have a telling effect on how the child views himself or herself across all the dimensions of being human. The truth is that where the parent is at in terms of those eight dimensions is all that they can offer their children. If the parent hates or is uncertain about physical appearance, struggles with emotional expression and is not receptive to how others are emotionally, feels socially inadequate or imposes socially on others, is sexually repressed or obsessed with sex, feels intellectually inferior or superior, behaviourally feels inadequate or relies on others for care, has little or no consciousness of her or his amazing creativity and spiritually doubts that there is any deeper meaning to life, this psychological safeguarding of Self will have profound effects on the child's expression of Self across these different dimensions of Self-expression.

Parents' psychological safety

Of course, when a parent truly consciously occupies and celebrates her or his unique physicality, is comfortable with both emotional expression and receptivity, is socially confident, sees sexuality as passion for life, feels intellectually able, and has a sense of endless creative potential and has personal experience of spiritual connection, what this parent offers her or his children is endless possibilities. By the time a child reaches pre-school age, that child will either be in survival mode or consciously thriving. Pre-school and primary school teachers are in a powerful position to identify the child who is struggling and the child who is thriving, but they too, like parents, can respond to the child only from where they are at in themselves.

The importance of having somebody in the school who has examined and continues to examine her or his life, is trained to identify the unconscious and conscious dimensions of human behaviour, is in a conscious psychological safety place to connect deeply with the child who is surviving – or indeed thriving – and with where the child's parents and pre-school teacher are in themselves, and has an in-depth understanding and experience of nurturing, and is in awe of the unconscious psychological safeguards created by both adults and children, is rarely to be found within pre-school, primary and second-level schools. Certainly, it is important that the teacher relates consciously with the child and each parent, but then there is no guarantee of that given that teachers are not obliged to reflect on their lives to date.

It is all the more important that there is a conscious relationship professional who takes charge of the situation where a child presents with challenging behaviours. The word challenging is good because the level of consciousness of the teacher and relationship professional will determine how they will respond – protectively or openly – in the face of the child's and the parents' protective behaviours. The fact of the matter is that the level of psychological safety of the relationship professional, the teacher and the school leader will determine how much progress is made in response to the cries for help from the child and from the parents. Any one of us can provide care for another only to the extent that we provide conscious care for ourselves.

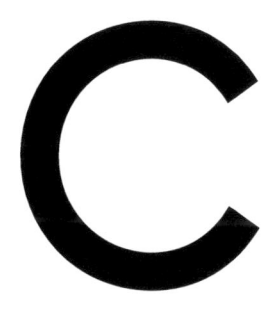

Chapter Six:
Teachers' Psychological Safety First

- Digging Deep
- Teachers' Psychological Safeguarding
- Students' Safety vs Safeguarding Solutions
- Teachers' Safety vs Safeguarding Solutions

Digging deep

Next to parents, teachers have a huge influence not just on a child's educational progress but, in many ways, even more so on the child's emotional and social development. How a teacher responds to each individual pupil in the classroom has a telling effect, not only on the degree to which each child retains natural curiosity, love of learning and risk-taking but also on whether the child will experience the psychological safety to use his or her intellectual potential consciously or will be pushed into unconscious usage.

A fact that many educators are not conscious of is that is what is unconscious in them, no matter how well intentioned they are, will be transmitted to the student, and the student's unconscious safeguarding responses may remain a continuing block, not only to educational progress but also to psychosocial development.

As already mentioned, teachers make more eye contact and ask more questions of children they consider 'bright' compared to those they have relegated to not having academic potential. Why is that so? Is it that those teachers, albeit unconsciously, have fears of failure or an addiction to success or to what others say about them – the school principal, colleagues, parents? Whatever the sources of their favouritism, teachers deserve the opportunity to examine what is secretly happening in the practise of their profession, so that they can find the psychological safety to consciously graduate to enjoying teaching as creative play rather than as a form of self-validation. The question a-begging here is that given that their safeguarding responses are unconscious, how are they to become conscious of their hidden fears?

I recall speaking to a large gathering of school principals on this issue and asking the question: "When you walk around the corridors of your school and you hear, for example, a teacher shouting at students, do you stop, listen to what is happening and realise that that teacher is unconsciously shouting out for help – not only to manage the challenging behaviours of some students, but even more so, for the psychological safety to bring to consciousness unresolved traumas experienced in his or her earlier life which are as actively present in the classroom as when the original lessening of presence, or ridiculing or criticism occurred?" The possibilities are multiple; we could guess and guess but only the teacher himself or herself can tell exactly what occurred in his or her life-story. What is apparent from the shouting behaviour is that the teacher's own past abandonment experiences are very much active in the present classroom.

There was a telling silence to my question, a silence that became even more pronounced when I added: "And when you as a principal walk by and decide to take no action on the teacher's shouting, then who realises for you that your passivity is shouting out even more loudly about what is unconsciously psychologically safeguarded in you that wants to come into consciousness?" Again, let me repeat, age, status, education, gender, wealth, or success – none of these is an index of psychological safety. The psychological safety principal would automatically know how to respond to the teacher who shouts at the students, or indeed, to a colleague principal who avoids taking action in response to a teacher's aggression towards students. The conscious principal would ensure care for both the students *and* the teacher. He would enquire of the students how they felt and what unmet needs they had in their relationship with the teacher, with the principal and, more delicately, with their parents. He would enquire of the teacher how is it that he is shouting at the children and how can he best support him to resolve what is happening for him when teaching.

It cannot be left to parents, teachers or principals to foster psychological safety for consciousness of our amazing nature to emerge. Nurturing individual psychological safety is also the responsibility of educationalists and politicians and – when conscious – to create a culture that provides psychological, social and intellectual safety, as well as the values and educational opportunities that maintain conscious expression of all that is awesome about our nature, rather than the much more prevalent repression and suppression of our immense capacity to thrive. It is a tragedy that so much of our innate potential is applied to unconsciously surviving all the different threats we encounter in our different holding worlds.

A story will illustrate. My wife and I used to frequent a beautifully situated restaurant overlooking a bay. We had got to know the lady owner who managed the front of house, and had made some acquaintance with her husband who was the chef. We had met her teenage daughters but not her younger child, aged six years. On one particular Sunday we went with a friend to lunch and, as usual, were guided to a sitting room area, seated and provided with menus and wine list. The room was full – certainly over 20 people. As we were perusing the menu, the six-year-old daughter approached me, caught my eye and declared "I hate school." I asked her name and enquired gently "How is it that you hate school?" The child answered "Well, Mr… expects us to have manners but he has no manners himself." When I enquired how it was that the teacher had no manners, the child replied "Well, he shouts all the time."

At this point the child's mother came and reproached the child "You must not be talking to the guests, come away now." I quickly intervened and said "Actually, your daughter and I are having a conversation and I would appreciate if you left us to it." Now the mother knew me of old and we always had friendly contact and she left her daughter there with me. The daughter told me more of the reasons she hated school but the recurring theme was her teacher shouting at her and at the other pupils. Later on, when paying the bill, the child's mother remarked to me "Tony, you know she is a bit of a drama queen." My response was that I was concerned for her daughter and when any six-year-old child says she hates school it rings alarm bells for me. I alerted her that I felt a crisis was imminent. I did add that I had equal concern for the teacher involved, and if any crisis did occur, I encouraged her to talk *with* the teacher not *to or at* and likewise *with* her daughter.

When we talk *with*, we are being non-judgmental but, nonetheless, authentic about bringing attention to the child's trauma and requesting support in responding to it. When we talk *to*, we tend to attack or advise, thereby disempowering, and when we talk *at*, we preach and adopt a superior moral stance – all unconscious psychological safeguarding responses which, unwittingly, serve only to exacerbate the crisis. I did say to the mother that I would be returning in a month's time, not just to dine but also to enquire of the school situation for her daughter.

On return to the restaurant one month later, out popped the daughter! When I enquired how things were for her, she looked me straight in the eyes and replied "Things are fine" and went off about her business – no need for chat this time! Later, her mother told me that following my last visit – which was on a Sunday – the child had returned to the school on the Monday and there had been no apparent distress until the following Monday when she refused point blank to go to school. When the mother patiently enquired "How is it that you don't want to go to school?" the daughter sharply replied "Teacher told me not to come to school on Monday." The story that emerged was that the child had been caught chatting with a schoolmate during class and the teacher had roared "Don't come to school on Monday; do you hear me, don't come to school on Monday."

Tone of voice can cause much misery for anyone, but especially for children. How creative and wise for the child to dig her heels in solidly about not going to school on that Monday. Her mother remembered my suggestion to talk *with* rather than *at* the teacher when she went to meet him, and explained that her daughter was terrified of going to school because of his shouting at her and at other classmates, and that she was requesting his support in making it psychologically safe for the child to return to school. To his credit, the teacher responded proactively and declared "I didn't realise what I was doing, I had no idea I was terrifying the children." He offered to come to the house to talk with the child, apologise and assure her that he would not shout again.

The word realise tells it all. Once the person sees matters with 'real eyes' – conscious psychological safety – he or she will engage in conscious and proactive action, benefiting both Self and others. If the mother in this case had coerced her daughter into returning to school, the child, wisely and intelligently, would have escalated her protective responses. The fact that the mother spoke *with* the teacher created the psychological safety for the teacher to come to consciousness of his protective shouting and decide to take the conscious and proactive response to resolve the matter.

Many teachers unconsciously assume that when a child breaks the rules, or throws a tantrum, or refuses to obey, that the source of their reaction of annoyance or irritability or crossness or shouting is the child's challenging behaviour. But the truth is that the child's behaviour is communicating something that is going on in the child and is calling for the psychological safety to give expression to what is troubling her. Likewise, the teacher's responses – whether unconsciously reactive or consciously proactive – are reflective of the teacher's inner world; protective reactions are reflective of hidden fears within the teacher that are 'shouting out' for resolution. As long as a teacher believes that it is the children's behaviours that are driving him or her wild, or causing anger, no resolution is possible.

In the case of the child above, it would appear that, at first, nobody was listening to her distress. Mother diluted it by referring to her daughter as 'a drama queen', father did not appear to feature at all, teacher was acting protectively, and the school principal was not offering support and help to the teacher. Marvellously, the child managed to pick the only psychologist in the restaurant waiting room to tell her tale. One wonders if I had not been in a position to listen to and champion the child what would have transpired. The good news was that Mr… came to be the child's 'favourite' teacher. What a gift to everyone concerned that child proved to be.

As already mentioned, there is the commonly held belief that the future of society lies with children. Nothing is further from the truth. The future of society lies with adults because children have to survive us and, unless we come into consciousness of the safeguarding strategies we have created to survive our own childhoods and make that shift from surviving to thriving, from dependence to independence, from hiding to emerging, then children will continue to suffer in the face of our unresolved traumas.

Teacher training needs to incorporate the inner course of creating the psychological safety to bring to light what lies in the unconscious, and identifying and supporting the conscious actions needed for emergence. This inner journey is the longest, most painful, but yet most exciting journey teachers can take; it is more painful when that journey is not undertaken. The groundwork needs to be done during teacher-training years but it is important that the school culture continues to support this ongoing journey of knowing oneself and finding conscious governorship of oneself. When such an enlightened ethos is not present in the school everybody suffers.

Clearly, school principals play a crucial role here and the provision of psychological safety opportunities for their continued examination of their lives is critical to both the creation and maintenance of psychological safety within their schools. Indeed, the provision of psychological safety for both students and teachers to be able to voice their fears, worries, struggles, feelings of depression, bullying experiences, pressure to conform, unrealistic expectations and labelling is essential for radiant mind and fearlessness to re-emerge.

Each of us as adults will have had during our school days incidents that either inspired us or caused us to 'expire'; sadly, the latter is often the more frequent experience. One memory that has persisted with me is when on entering sixth class in primary school, the male teacher greeted me with the statement "You may have been first in class up to now but you won't get first in my class." I can still feel the hurt and injustice of it but how can an 11-year-old child confront a teacher with "Sir, how is it that you're saying that; is it that you never got first yourself? I find what you're saying to be threatening." There is no doubt that any attempt to stand by myself in the situation would have provoked even more threatening responses from the teacher. What is even sadder for me to remember is that I did not reveal what this teacher had said to me either to any other teacher or to my parents. Obviously, there was not the psychological safety to speak the truth in either the holding world of the school or home.

Interestingly, at some point during that school year there was a school inspection and the inspector when examining the class asked quite a difficult question on poetry to which I was the only one to give an answer and, as it happened, the correct answer. I overheard the inspector saying to the teacher "You've got a bright lad there" and the teacher responding "He shows a bright spark now and then." One wonders what was unconscious in that teacher and how many other children had been affected by his hidden fears. It was sad for the teacher that nobody noticed his secret plight and sad for students, like myself, who in a clever – unconscious genius – response created the psychological safeguarding of doubting my ability. If you don't show your ability then you avoid the pain of being diminished or scorned!

Teachers' psychological safeguarding

In any profession – such as parenting, teaching, medicine, psychology or business – there are individuals whose real potential lies hidden. There are many reasons for this being the case. It does not help when such individuals are labelled as 'bad'. Individuals come into a profession with a certain level of emotional, social and intellectual consciousness, and the measure of their professional effectiveness rests on the psychological solidity of their inner world. No teacher wants to block the progress of any child, but unresolved insecurities and fears can lead to responding in ways that are unconsciously safeguarding of one's Self but are detrimental to the child's progress. When I reflect on my own teaching days, I cringe at many of my responses to the children in my classroom. Ironically, the students regarded me as a 'nice' teacher but I know now that my low self-esteem meant that I was not there for the students in the conscious psychological safety ways they deserved.

As a teacher, the extent to which you find conscious psychological safety for yourself is the measure of how well you can hold each individual student in the classroom. The presence of that psychological safety also determines your responses to the unconscious safeguarding behaviours that, inevitably, get exhibited by students inside and outside the classroom.

It is not only the teachers who bring their psychological safeguards into the classroom but so too do the students and, indirectly, the parents of the students. It takes considerable psychological safety to withstand troubling behaviours exhibited by students and by parents – troubling behaviours such as overly demanding expectations of achievement. Parents too have their unresolved insecurities and these can be projected on to their children and their children's teachers.

Teachers who operate from an inner place of psychological safety know that students are not out to make life difficult for them or for their fellow students. On the contrary, these teachers know that the students are using psychological safeguards, rather than psychological safety responses, as ways of drawing attention to how difficult life is for them. Certainly, a conscious cooperation between teachers and parents is desirable in order to understand

and respond compassionately to the inner turmoil of the young person. Teachers who possess a felt sense of psychological safety in themselves are in a place to set clear and definite boundaries around their right to teach and, particularly, around their right to respect for themselves and others in the classroom in the face of troubling behaviours that threaten these boundaries. In order to do this effectively, the individual teacher would benefit when school managers and colleagues are also in a psychological safety place.

Boundaries get established when teachers take action *for Self* and *not against* students. Easy to say, but it takes considerable psychological safety and practice to put into action. It is for this reason that teachers, vice-principals and principals need ongoing opportunities to deepen their understanding of themselves, colleagues, parents and students, to develop conscious management strategies and to enhance their motivation to teach. It appears that up to 40% of new teachers lose their motivation and enthusiasm within one year of starting to teach. Such a statistic suggests that they were not adequately prepared for the realities of classroom life and the truth that teaching is primarily about relationship – relationship with oneself and with the students. Of course, a love of knowledge and teaching are necessary, but when there is not present a conscious psychosocial readiness to teach or to learn, motivation quickly flies out of the school window.

A sound perspective on the issues of teachers having challenges in teaching is crucial. There are no statistics to indicate how many teachers feel fulfilled or disillusioned. It is not easy for any one of us to admit to experiencing professional difficulties and personal fears and doubts. The suspicion is that there are a significant number of teachers who are living lives of quiet desperation. Some indication of the latter is the unprecedented rise in teachers taking early retirement or leaving the profession on stress and health grounds. But it is important that the high numbers of teachers whose practice is excellent are not forgotten in the current drive to resolve the challenge of those teachers who are struggling.

When politicians use the term 'underperforming' teachers and describe teaching as 'a well-protected' profession, they unwittingly exhibit a lack of understanding and compassion. No teacher wants to go into school every day of their working lives dreading the day and 'losing it' with students. The fact is that teachers have not been provided with an honourable way out of teaching or the opportunity to re-train and transfer their knowledge and skills on to other professional careers. Furthermore, the training of teachers requires serious revision, and passing the buck of responsibility to school boards of management is unconscious 'underperformance' on the part of the Department of Education. Indeed, it is essential that nobody is scapegoated in attempts to resolve this serious educational issue. It is a matter of the wellbeing of teachers who are troubled in themselves and, as a result, being troubling in their relationships with their students. Whether or not an effective solution is found will depend on whether an approach is adopted that is sensitive, non-judgmental and caring – conscious psychological safety.

Students' safety vs safeguarding solutions

Alongside parenting, teaching is also a highly responsible profession. If parenting is rocket science so too is teaching. As indicated, many teachers are experiencing considerable difficulties within classrooms and staffrooms, and morale can be low in some schools. Some teachers are of the opinion that it is students' difficult and undisciplined behaviours that are the sources of their stress. While it is true that there are students who present with extremely challenging behaviours in schools and classrooms, the stress of teachers unconsciously arises from within themselves and from an educational system that does not offer support and back-up systems to empower teachers to take conscious action for themselves in the face of the difficult reactions of students.

It helps when teachers are in a place to view students' troubling behaviours as being completely about the students concerned. When teachers personalise students' behaviours, with a hidden purpose, they pile up challenges for themselves. Staying separate from students' protective behaviours and taking definite action for themselves in the face of threats to their wellbeing, and their right to teach, are essential conscious emergences. When teachers *react* rather than *proact* they will blame the students for the anger and frustration they are experiencing and will tend to punish 'undesirable' behaviours.

Punishment never works (Humphreys, 1998) because it does not target the hidden reasons why students behave as they do. Punishment also lowers self-esteem and further interrupts the relationship between teacher and student – a sure recipe for the escalation of the students' and, indeed, the teachers' unconscious safeguarding responses. It is frequently the case that the very behaviour a teacher employs to correct a student's behaviour is more challenging than the one being corrected. When a student's challenging behaviour is met with a challenging reaction on the part of the teacher, no resolution of the troubled situation can emerge. The reality is that the teacher is shouting out for psychological safety as much as the student who is troubled and troublesome.

Some teachers may claim that their verbal aggression or use of the sophisticated put-down create fear and consequent quiet in the classroom. But teachers who want students to be afraid of them require more psychological safety holding than the students they are attempting to control. The central question is: who in the school system is there to offer these teachers the psychological safety and support they require to examine and resolve their own unconscious safeguarding and threatening responses? Ultimately, it is the individual responsibility of each teacher to become consciously Self-reliant but it helps enormously when there are structures in place to support teachers in their efforts to reach consciousness. Indicators of consciousness include: self-regard, emotional expressiveness, realisation of one's own genius, independence, separateness and strong boundaries around one's unique presence. The establishment of this conscious interior solidity and psychological safety is the desire of all adults, but it is a long and difficult road to travel, particularly if you have encountered many emotional, social and intellectual setbacks during childhood and adolescence and there is little psychological safety present in the here-and-now.

As a teacher and lecturer myself, I have found it helpful to *notice* my own safeguarding responses to students' troubling behaviours and to *understand* the deeper nature and intentions of my reactions. For example, if a response of annoyance arises in me because a student is not understanding what I have explained several times, I now know that the annoyance is within myself and not caused by the student, and that a performance dependence is dogging my heels. The deeper personal issue is the confusion of my presence with performance – a not uncommon experience for those of us who have been reared in a culture that is performance and success driven.

The opportunities for me are to *own* my fear, to see its psychological safeguarding *intention* to protect my wholeness in the eyes of the student, and to be mindful of the deeper purpose, which is for me to unconditionally accept myself and let go of the confusion of my presence with academic performance. The annoyance is a creative safeguarding response as I put the pressure on the students to understand, thereby making them responsible for the *real* action of understanding myself. It is sad that when I do not see what is really happening I miss the chance to emerge more and deprive the students of the opportunity to deepen their knowledge of the subject being taught. Furthermore, I create psychological unsafety in my relationship with the students and they are likely to stop asking questions or look for clarification. All in all, there is no substitute for the real thing of gradually finding psychological safety and support to take conscious responsibility for myself.

Teachers' safety vs safeguarding solutions

The word discipline comes from the word disciple and means follower of good practice. The move by Departments of Education in some countries to discipline 'poor' teachers is welcome, but the nature of the language used and the disciplining procedures suggested fail to demonstrate understanding and compassion. Without compassion and understanding – the basis of psychological safety - there can be no effective resolution of what is a complex issue. For example, one response to the language being used is that in the same way that there are no 'bad' students – just unconscious psychological safeguarding behaviour – there are no 'poor' teachers, but there can be poor and inadequate teaching. Furthermore, the traditional ways of disciplining have not worked for students and are highly unlikely to work with teachers.

My own experience of the teaching profession is that no teacher ever wants to be 'incompetent' or block the progress of their students. In the same way that the difficult and troubling responses of students in the classroom are crying out for some conscious adult to spot how difficult life is for them, a teacher's unconscious psychological safeguarding behaviours also have the purpose of drawing attention to how difficult life is for them. Certainly, it has been an injustice to teachers and other students to keep in the classroom those young people who are not psychosocially ready for school learning; indeed, it is an unwitting neglect of the troubled students themselves to not provide the opportunities for resolution of the troubling aspects of their lives – whether in homes, schools or communities. It is equally an unconscious safeguarding to have a teacher who 'hates' teaching, is seriously struggling with discipline, or who has high performance anxiety, or is burnt out, or deeply personally troubled, going into class each day.

Students need teachers who possess a high level of conscious psychological safety, who feel good about themselves and their students, who establish fair and definite boundaries around their right to teach and students' right to learn. Teachers who are in a conscious secure place ask for help and support when these are required. But it can be the case that there is not psychological safety in the staffroom for a teacher to reach out for interpersonal and professional support. The reality is that when a teacher is struggling with teaching and classroom management, it can be the situation that the principal involved may be struggling with their professional briefs.

Consciousness is a matter of the degree – the ripeness – of how much you know and give expression to the fullness of your unique presence. Some people in the teaching profession – staff and management alike – can cynically respond to this definition of maturity as 'navel gazing' or 'soft stuff' but the reality is that the deepest drive of each adult is to consciously know Self and take responsibility for one's actions. How can students be consciously self-reliant without conscious self-reliance being modelled by their parents and teachers? It is understandable that cynicism arises from fear and that it is very threatening for any one of us – not just teachers – to examine our own responses, particularly when there is not peer psychological safety and support to do so.

Nevertheless, personal accomplishments are the basis of professional accomplishments and it is a secret drive in each adult

– and not only those who have management roles within homes, classrooms, staffrooms, communities, churches and state bodies – to seek, when psychological safety is present, the support they need to resolve the unconscious psychological blocks to their being affective and effective at personal, interpersonal and professional levels.

The procedures for dealing with the teacher whose teaching is falling short of what would be professionally expected needs also to address the issue of the school principal's level of personal and professional psychological safety and his or her competence to assess the particular work of a teacher in a particular subject. When struggling, principals also need peers to turn to for help and psychology safety, and teachers who are at the mercy of a principal who requires help and support need to be able to go outside the school for such help – maybe to the school inspector assigned to the school or to an independent psychological professional service.

I also have considerable concern that the discipline procedures being adopted are focusing too much on the teacher's competence in the classroom and not on the teacher's personal effectiveness. My clinical experience is that teachers who struggle with their teaching are suffering internally and it is the resolution of the latter that releases the energy, drive, ambition and commitment to becoming professionally competent.

The crucial issue in responding to the troubled and troubling behaviours of teachers or principals or students is that it is done in conscious psychological safety ways that are sensitive to the person's biographical story, and that understanding and compassion are the driving behaviours towards effective teaching, managing and learning. Finally, in terms of prevention – meaning to stop the coming of – the training of teachers seriously needs to be reviewed, as indicated already.

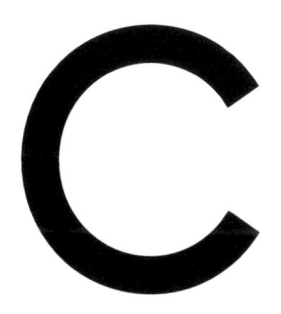

Chapter Seven:
Psychological Safety vs Safeguarding Schools

- Setting the Scene
- Being Affective in Teaching
- Seven Psychological Safeguards in Education
- Teaching to the Test
- Tone of Voice Speaks Volumes

Setting the scene

It is said that the eyes are the window to the soul, and how the teacher perceives each student and how each student perceives the teacher are major contributing factors to the ethos of a classroom. This is true also for staffrooms. The fundamental need of a student is to belong – to a family, to a classroom, to a school, to a community, to a country. A teacher has a need to belong also – to Self, to a partner, to a staff, to a social group, to the school, community and country. Both students and teachers are often hurt and disappointed due to an underbelonging (diminishment of individuality) or an overbelonging (suffocation of individuality) or no belonging (annihilation of individuality). This need to belong is met by an 'I' to 'I' relationship wherein the teacher recognises and affirms the individual and unique presence of each student and the student likewise for the teacher.

But unless the teacher and student first belong to Self and inhabit their own interiority – an essential consciousness – classroom conflict will inevitably emerge. Such conflict is the creative opportunity to reflect on the nature of belonging within both teacher and student and the classroom. Both teacher and student require the psychological safety to realise that person comes before teaching and learning and that relationship is not jeopardised by differences or behavioural difficulties that arise in the classroom. The teacher's knowing of Self and knowing of each student (psychological safety teaching) is the basis of affective and effective teaching. How this might be achieved within schools is discussed below under the following headings:

- Being affective in teaching
- Seven psychological safeguards in education
- Teaching to the test
- Tone of voice speaks volumes

Being affective in teaching

Being *effective* is the ambition of organisations in all fields, but what is not often appreciated is that being *affective* is an essential aspect of being effective. The mind without affect is not mind at all. Equally the practice of a profession is not practice at all without heart. The verb *to affect* means to influence and the verb *to effect* means to cause, to get a result. It appears to me that these two words are inextricably linked; they are bedfellows that when used together have the potential to bring about powerful and continuing emergence of our conscious ingenious psychological safety nature.

A school's culture that is not affective in nature, in that it does not encompass concern for each individual staff member, student and parent, can act like a dark force in the lives of those exposed to it. Heads of schools, especially male heads, have typically referred to affective qualities as the 'soft' aspect of management, but it is ironic how 'hard' it is for men to embrace an affective approach in their professional lives. There is no mystery to this reality as males, when young, often are ridiculed, diminished or laughed at when they express such emotions as fear, sadness, hurt or depression and, indeed, love and affection. Wisely, they reduce experiencing such threats by ingeniously repressing these emergency and welfare emotions – unconscious psychological safeguarding. The irony of it is that when the school culture supports teachers to lead with both head and heart the teachers are far more balanced and effective, and they create a psychological safety environment where a sense of belonging and belief in them are felt by their students.

Where does the fear of being affective begin? The recognition of the importance of being able to perceive and express an affective experience is a relatively recent phenomenon. There are still cultures that do not value and often punish the perception and expression of emotions. In many workplaces such a taboo exists, as it does in many schools, third-level educational institutions and health services. Within families – and each family is a unique subculture – there can be a ban on emotional expression – more so for male children. Children frequently get the messages 'don't feel what you are feeling', 'don't feel too deeply, don't be so intense', 'feelings are dangerous', 'feelings can lead you to be out of control', 'you are weak when you show feelings'.

But feelings do not disappear because children are told not to have them. Feelings creatively arise; they are there to give expression to needs or the reality of unmet needs. When children or adults repress or suppress their feelings – powerful and creative psychological safeguarding responses – to the dangers of emotional expression, these buried feelings will find substitute means of expression such as substance addictions or self-harming or passive-aggression or illness or emotional outbursts that appear to happen out of the blue.

In terms of the wellbeing of children, and their adult roles in the future, it is in a psychological safety accompaniment by parents, child-minders and teachers that will allow them to express their honest feelings. The most powerful way to encourage and support children to be emotionally expressive is for the adults to be in a psychological safety place so that they express openly how they are feeling in ways that they take ownership of what arises in them – feelings, thoughts and actions. Children necessarily take their cues from adults, and it is of very great benefit when the significant adult males and females in their lives model emotional expression and receptivity.

Emotional *expression* is about revealing feelings as they arise with the realisation that these are *of, belong to and are for you*; such adult realisations lead to children owning their feelings and communicating the met or unmet needs that give rise to the welfare or emergency emotions. On the other hand, emotional *receptivity* is about the other person being open to listening to another's emotional expression while holding the realisation that what is being emotionally expressed is of, belongs to and is for the person who is expressing the emotion – either a welfare or emergency emotion.

As seen, it has not been the practice for schools to create a culture for teachers and other members of staff to 'know themselves' before embarking on their teaching or leadership responsibilities. To 'know Self' is to appreciate that every feeling, thought, image, dream and action that arises in us is about us and is calling for us take conscious care of Self. If this is true for us, it is also true for everybody else. People lose out when psychological safety opportunities are not provided on an ongoing basis for individual managers and their charges to know Self in the ways described. It is not a simple process because we live in a society that has fostered co-dependence rather than independence. The benefits of consciousness and being consciously self-reliant and independent for systems and their members are huge. When opportunities for the development of consciousness are not provided, systems experience great losses and their members can often have a life of misery.

Seven psychological safeguards in education

The wellbeing of teachers has not been a priority in schools, even though it substantially determines a teacher's affectiveness and effectiveness. The wellbeing of students has also often been sacrificed to an overfocus on head matters and inadequate attention to heart matters. Furthermore, the unconscious psychological safeguarding behaviours of teachers, parents and students need to be understood as mirroring the inner and outer turmoil of these individuals who are troubled and troubling. Relationship lies at the heart of effective teaching where the person of both teacher and student does not come under threat by a results-driven culture, curriculum demands, examinations, failure, success and other unconscious safeguarding responses.

The seven psychological safeguards that commonly occur within educational settings are:

- Education without relationship

- Knowledge without psychological safety
- Teaching without separateness
- Learning without individualisation
- Failure without fearlessness
- Discipline without understanding
- Achievement not seen as always present

Education without relationship

The teacher's relationship with Self lies at the heart of being an effective teacher. Conscious genius relationship operates from both heart and head, manifesting the essential masculine qualities: drive, ambition, order, determination, establishment of boundaries, problem-solving and solid firmness; and the essential feminine qualities: love, nurture, kindness, understanding, support, gentleness, compassion and empathy. Centuries ago, the Chinese sage Lao Tzu echoed the wisdom of being consciously ingenious: "To know Self is wise, to know another is learned." It is considerably fearful for many people, not just teachers, to give priority to their own relationship with Self. The absence of that knowing of Self, inevitably, affects how teachers relate to students.

Everybody wants to re-examine their lives but will only do so when there is psychological safety. Rumi, the Sufi poet of ancient times, put it well: "A person becomes an adult only when they take (conscious) responsibility for Self and for their own actions." It is a sad irony that schools, teachers and many of their students unconsciously place a lot more emphasis on school examinations than on the crucial re-examination of Self. Aristotle brings the seriousness of that irony to light when he wrote: "A life unexamined is a life not lived." What Aristotle missed was that, as children, we very thoroughly examined our lives and created safeguarding solutions in the face of adverse experiences and maintained our radiance in the face of unconditional love. It is, then, more accurate to say "a life not re-examined is a life not lived." Not surprisingly, when the Self re-examination is a daily practice, school and other examinations are seen as creative play rather than as ways of getting approval.

Knowledge without psychological safety

Knowledge is power but when held without psychological safety it can be a terrifying weapon wielded by those who unconsciously use it to control, manipulate or be superior to others. It is not an uncommon phenomenon to encounter professional people who, though highly educated, act unconsciously in superior, arrogant and dismissive ways. Knowledge or status or education or professional position are no indices of consciousness and it is often the case that individuals who have been fortunate enough to have had educational opportunities, but who have not been given opportunities for re-examining their lives, are put in leadership positions.

In a psychological safety culture it is integral to the training of all professionals – parents, teachers, school principals, psychologists, psychiatrists, medical doctors, managers, politicians – that they be provided with the opportunities to evaluate their present level of consciousness and given the psychological support and resources to pursue resolution of their fears and insecurities. It is an unwitting disservice to them and to those who are accountable to them to put them in positions of power because they are qualified in a particular field of knowledge. The more adults are in a conscious place to act in psychological safety ways in their knowledge fields, the more children and society benefit from them.

Teaching without separateness

The unconscious safeguarding behaviour of teaching without separateness causes great confusion in classrooms and staffrooms. There are four dimensions to separateness: teachers are not what they do; students are not what they do; students' responses to teachers' teaching are about the students and are not saying anything about the teachers; and teachers' responses to students are completely about the teachers! When teachers are unconsciously enmeshed with their teaching, they evaluate their worth and value through it, and they will put pressure on themselves and on their students to reinforce their psychological safeguarded sense of identity. A person's value lies in their unique and sacred presence and has absolutely nothing to do with behaviour – a realisation that comes with conscious psychological safety and resulting separateness.

As children, many of us wisely discerned that our worth lay in such behaviours as our school performance or examination results or our 'good' actions; the consequence is that we developed a psychological safeguarded identity in order to reduce the threat of rejection. If this creative identity protection in students and teachers remains unconscious and manifests itself in fear of failure, performance anxiety, success addiction, attention-deficits and other such manifestations, then classrooms become psychological safeguarded rather than psychological safety environments.

In a school culture where separateness is active, it becomes a freeing experience for teachers to consciously realise that their own responses are about themselves and that students' responses are about the students. The teacher who reacts to students' challenging responses will find teaching very difficult and is unlikely to be effective in classroom management. The teacher who consciously proacts from the secure place of reading the students' behaviour as being about the student will create the psychological safety opportunities for the students to reveal their inner turmoil and their unmet emotional, social and intellectual needs, while maintaining definite boundaries around care of Self, their right to teach and the wellbeing and the right to learn of the other students.

Within a psychological safety school setting, the teachers who come to own their own responses can take the response of not being separate as an opportunity to deepen their knowing of themselves and, for example, can readily express regret and admit to a student "What I did yesterday was because of my own fears around responding to your difficult behaviour and I do regret it. What I would like is to understand the behaviour of yours I got annoyed with and offer any help and support that will resolve it for you."

Learning without individualisation

One of the most common complaints among students is the experience of anonymity in the school and in the classroom. Psychological safety to being present to the individuality of each student in a classroom is an essential antidote to this fourth unconscious safeguarding behaviour. It is interesting that when a teacher is present to his or her own unique presence, they automatically recognise the importance of marking the presence of each individual student in the classroom. Respecting and acknowledging individuality is about the affirmation of the sacred and unique presence of each student and the recognition, too, that each student brings a unique story of how he or she has managed to fashion ways of manifesting that individuality, sometimes in the face of great threat or tremendous pressure to conform, or competition and rivalry from siblings.

As illustrated already, it is extraordinary how children within their families find their own repertoire of behaviours that distinguish them from siblings. The psychological safety school and teachers are alert to this amazing individualising process and recognise it as the solid base on which to build a child's school learning. To ignore or dismiss the child's individualising process may result in a serious loss of motivation to cooperate with the teacher and the school curriculum. Calling students by their first names raises their Self-esteem as does noticing in an affirming and psychological safety way the unique presence of each student and what they uniquely bring to a classroom and to a school.

The psychological safety school culture practises a knowing that each student in a classroom has a different teacher, because when two unique people interact it is a unique experience. Another consciousness that psychological safety schools hold is that each student has a different story, a story of which the teacher will have little or no knowledge. For this reason, psychological safety teachers do not make assumptions, label and make academic, behavioural or social predictions about children.

Children deserve teachers who acknowledge their unique presence, their limitless possibilities, their cleverness in the ways they express their individuality and how their difference matters. The school culture that responds to students in these psychological safety ways very often becomes a life-line for children, particularly those who may be drowning in or struggling with the rapid and enveloping waters of rejection, neglect, criticism, comparison and family conflict. The influence that school and classroom cultures can have on a child's sense of Self is undocumented because teaching is predominately evaluated – and not very effectively – on a quantitative rather than a qualitative basis.

Failure without fearlessness

Failure and success are integral to learning, these two common experiences being intrinsic bedfellows to the whole adventure of learning. The fear of failure has become one of the greatest impediments to learning due to the sad experience of failure being punished and criticised and evoking disappointment in parents and teachers. Children, in response to the threats that surround failure, develop safeguarding responses that are designed to reduce the threats – responses that can be puzzling to parents and teachers, who, because of their own hidden fears of failure and addiction to success, are not in a conscious place to see the wood from the trees.

A typical response shown by children is avoidance of those subject areas where failure is likely to occur and be punished. It is very often for this reason that children hate mathematics because answers are either right or wrong. The psychological safety mathematics teacher puts the emphasis on the effort and the process, not the answer. Teachers who have not resolved their own issues around failure tend to place emphasis on the performance outcome. Avoidance is such a clever response to the threats that failure presents – with no effort, there can be no failure; with no failure, there can be no criticism.

Another ingenious safeguarding method children employ is 'always having to get it right', and they can put major pressure on themselves to bring that about. When things go against them, they cleverly, albeit unconsciously, become very upset and frenetic, even physically sick – all designed to offset threats around failure. Quite a common response to the fear of failure is to go for the average, thereby reducing parents' and teachers' expectations. The truth is that in terms of intellectual potential there are no 'average', 'slow', 'weak', 'dull' or 'bright' categories, such categorisations often mirroring the teacher's own fears of failure and are an attempt to reduce people's expectations.

Genius is a given that has long been confused with knowledge. Knowledge is an index of learning; limitless intelligence is a part of our nature. When a child shows a high knowledge of a particular subject – and it has been estimated that there are 101 different knowledge areas – this does not mean he or she has a higher intelligence than other children. Equally, when a child exhibits poor knowledge of a particular subject this does not mean his or her intelligence is low. It is the astute and conscious teacher who spots that children never stop learning, but what they are learning may not be relevant to the school curriculum while totally and creatively relevant to situations outside of the school.

Opportunities for parents and teachers to examine their responses to failure and success need to be integral to a school's culture so that their conflicts are not passed on to children. Children as young as six years of age complain of being 'stressed out' by tests, but it is not the tests that stress them, it is the serious attitudes that adults have around examinations. The first question that many adults ask when attending third-level courses is "Are there tests?" This question spills the beans on either their psychological safeguarding fear of failure or the protective development of the addiction to success.

When children are toddlers they are fearless around risk-taking. If children's innate love of learning and excitement around learning is to be restored as adults – particularly parents and teachers – ways need to be found to recover fearlessness around failure and replace addiction to success with seeing learning as a creative pursuit and not as a means of proving Self.

Discipline without understanding

Discipline is an important part of a school culture. The aim of all school discipline needs to be the promotion of psychological safety and boundaries. Discipline is not punishment. Punishment does not empower and it lowers Self-esteem. The use of punishment is an indication of an unconscious psychological safeguarding school culture. When a school's discipline policy is of a conscious psychological safety nature and actively endorses the realisation that everything that arises in a teacher – feelings, thoughts, actions, expectations, needs – belongs to that teacher, then the teacher will automatically proact in the face of a child's protective behaviours. In proacting the teacher will give loving consideration to what the troubling behaviour might be manifesting about the child's interior and exterior world. Only when the teacher has some understanding of why this student is 'acting out' or 'acting in' does he or she put a boundary in place so that the rights of all are considered – including the child exhibiting the protective behaviour.

A good definition of discipline is that it is about *creating psychological safety for* the person and rights of those individuals who have experienced violations and those who have unconsciously perpetrated the violations. The focus firstly is put on the person who has experienced violations and, secondly, on the person who has perpetrated the violations. Discipline means that people experience psychological safety when encountering violations by the creation of a response whereby the teacher, supported by school policy, takes *action for Self* rather than against the student who created the undisciplined behaviour.

For example, when a student disrupts a classroom, the teacher, from a place of understanding that the disruptive behaviour is arising from the student's inner and outer turmoil, makes a very definite request of the student to desist from the behaviour that is violating the teacher's right to teach and the right of the other students to learn. When the student is not in a place to cooperate with the request being made, the teacher may now resort to the psychological safety action of requesting the student to leave the classroom and report to the vice-principal. If the student refuses to comply, the teacher maintains calm and equilibrium and requests another student to go and ask the vice-principal for assistance in his or her efforts to gain the cooperation of the student who is both troubled and troubling.

During all of these interactions, the teacher does not break the relationship with the student; he or she continues to address the student by first name, maintains eye contact and sends direct and clear 'I-messages' to the student. In being proactive, the teacher models for the student the proaction he or she is hoping to elicit from the student. When a teacher 'loses it' with a student it is a case of 'fighting fire with fire', and there is little hope of a resolution of the conflict situation. Incidentally, the student who out of fear conforms when a teacher 'loses it' learns nothing from the situation and it is likely that the next display of troubling behaviour will be worse than the last. Furthermore, the inducement of fear is not discipline but unconscious psychological safeguarding control through threat. When the latter is the case the presence of a psychological safety school culture will support the teacher to address his or her own inner fears.

When the dust has settled – when the violated right has been reinstated – that is the end of the need for discipline in that situation. But later on, in a one-to-one interaction, the conscious teacher will kindly enquire of the student as to what was happening for him or her when engaging in the disruptive behaviour and will ask what help could be offered. All behaviour has intention and 'undisciplined' behaviour can have the intention of drawing attention to some inner (for example, low self-esteem) or outer (for example, bullying) adverse home experiences that the student is undergoing. The teacher who shows such concern is likely to gain the trust of the student and a greater level of cooperation.

Achievement not seen as always present

Success has become a widespread psychological safeguarding addiction in western society; the creative illusion is that achievement makes people important, and that those who are successful are superior to those who underachieve. As already indicated, many schools are results driven as is evident in classrooms where children who are high achievers are given more eye contact and asked more questions than those students who are academically underachieving. It is not just academic achievements that have become a means of gaining recognition; achievements in music, sport, art, politics, business are also heralded. There is no rest from strain and pressure for those who do not view their achievements with humility; they are only as good as their last achievement, and so there is a constant fear of falling off the pedestal. Achievements are wonderful experiences, but they are not a measure of a person's worth, intelligence and value. Genius is always present. Indeed, as demonstrated, achievement is also always present either in an unconscious safeguarding or psychological safety way.

There are many individuals who do not have the educational and other opportunities to realise their potential. This does not mean they are of any less value in society; a threatening situation of 'them and us' is created when certain achievements are lauded. The threats are two-fold: a possible backlash from those perceived as 'inferior' or 'less than', and 'burn-out' or despair from those who protectively confuse their sense of Self and their worth and value with what they do. Achievements are there to be enjoyed, not to be held on to. Psychological safety school cultures embrace failures and successes as integral to the passion and excitement of learning and appreciate the limitless range and type of achievements, either conscious or unconscious, that individuals necessarily and creatively develop.

Teaching to the test

Teaching and learning are separate issues, and a school's effectiveness emerges from the consciously expressed personal and professional qualities that make for teaching excellence. As seen, school and teacher effectiveness are typically measured by student test and examination results. It is both an undue pressure and a misuse of standardised tests and examinations to hold individual teachers accountable for their students' learning outcomes. There is a belief that schools can achieve miracles by treating parents as consumers, students as products and teachers as compliant workers who are expected to 'teach to the test' – strategies similar to the ones that resulted in the worst economic crash to hit the western world in 2008.

Teaching to the test takes the heart out of the school culture and is a sure way of extinguishing a love of teaching and learning. This practice continues despite the fact that standardised test publishers warn that the test measures student performance, not teacher effectiveness. The fall-out from this approach to teacher evaluation is, for example, as already indicated, that it is proving more and more difficult to hold on to long-serving experienced teachers and, for example, in the US 40-50% of young teachers are staying in the profession for only a maximum of five years.

As previously mentioned, the word education comes from the Greek verb *educe* – meaning to draw forth from within. The original teaching method of Socrates has been largely displaced by professional deference to received scholarly authority. By and large, students are taught how to take examinations but not to think, write or find their own individual path. Teaching is not about instilling knowledge; it is about having the skills to draw out qualities of human nature that are openly expressed in children's earlier years but somehow get buried under an avalanche of attention to scholastic achievements, unrealistic expectations, disinterest, criticisms, tests and examinations. The natural qualities that are often unconsciously repressed in teachers, and in their students, are curiosity, passion for knowledge, fearlessness, aliveness, spontaneity, ease with failure and success, eagerness to learn, expansiveness, creativity and belief. Certainly, equality of educational opportunity, individualised learning plans, portfolio references and cooperative learning are necessary accompaniments to the foregoing.

It is essential, too, for teachers to be well educated, well prepared and highly respected for what is a hugely challenging profession. School provision of ongoing personal reflection and professional development are also essential to teacher effectiveness. Perhaps the requirement of a Master's degree as a minimum qualification would help establish teaching as the respected and prestigious profession it deserves to be. However, the nature of a Master's qualification needs to be examined and the priority of continuing personal reflection (CPR) be an integral part of the degree.

Finland provides an example of a system of education which is not based on accountability via test scores but on responsibility, this approach resulting in Finland having one of the highest attaining school systems in the OECD. Over the past 40 years, Finland has developed a different educational system by improving and extending teacher training by minimising student testing. Students are not given any standardised tests until the end of high school. These tests are drawn up by their own teachers – by individualising learning programmes; by emphasising cooperative, as opposed to competitive, learning; by the development of each student as an intelligent, active and creative person; and by emphasising responsibility and trust before accountability.

These psychological safety schools are creatively designed to meet the emotional, social, physical and academic needs of students, beginning at an early age. Finnish teachers are sensitive to not holding students back or labelling them as 'failing' because of consciousness that such responses increase student failure, reduce student motivation and increase social inequality. The story of Finland's educational achievement – from which performance-focused schools could benefit – is outlined in a must-read book by Pasi Sahlberg titled *What Can the World Learn from Educational Change in Finland?* (2011).

Tone of voice speaks volumes

Much of people's distress, particularly of children, arises in response to the tone of voice used by others. Many individuals are not conscious of the tone of voice they use but nonetheless, conscious or not, some psychological intervention is required for them to own what belongs to them. Contrary to what many people believe, tone of voice arises from an internal emotional place of either solidity or turmoil. When it is the former it communicates love, equality, openness, optimism, genuineness, sincerity, spontaneity, clarity and confidence. When it arises from inner turmoil, it can communicate either in an acting-out way – aggression, irritability, impatience, tetchiness, dismissiveness, arrogance, control, dominance, hostility, threat, tension; or in an acting-in way – fearfulness, pessimism, passivity, sadness, uncertainty, and indecisiveness.

The more common belief is that it is somebody else who triggers the particular tone of voice used. The truth is that what comes from each of us is about us, and it is a clever unconsciously developed psychological safeguarding manoeuvre to blame somebody else for our own responses. But a psychological safeguarding reaction never leads to a resolution of the underlying insecurity that gives rise to the protective tone of voice. Tone of voice at all times reveals – is a mirror of – our interiority.

It is an interesting exercise to brainstorm the possible tones of voice that are either used by or encountered from others. Of course, having identified one's own repertoire from the list below it behoves one to detect the inner source of the tones, particularly when they are of a safeguarding nature. The word tone is an anagram for the word note, and for the development of conscious psychological safety school cultures, and the wellbeing both of teachers and students, a key challenge for each of us is to find the psychological safety to consciously take note of tone of voice.

In brainstorming it is important to distinguish between the physical properties and the emotional intentions of the tone of voice. For example, when I say "your tone of voice is hard" I am defining its physical sound but when I say "your tone of voice is cross" I am alluding to its possible emotional intention to convey anger. I say 'possible' because it is crucial to check on an assumption and not presume to read another's behaviour. A conscious enquiry would be "I am wondering how you are feeling as you speak with me?"

It is useful then to brainstorm two lists, one conveying what the tone sounds like and the other its possible emotional intention.

A tone of voice may sound: light, heavy, squeaky, deep, high-pitched, low-pitched, deep-throated, bellowing, whimpering, earthy, sharp, firm, flat, soft, kind, well-modulated or full.

In terms of an unconscious or conscious emotional intention, you may experience a tone of voice as: cross, anxious, fearful, sad, depressed, joyful, chirpy, tentative, threatening, insistent, cutting, kind, gentle, tender, confident, indecisive, patronising, manipulative, domineering, rigid, seductive, flirtatious, erotic, mean, serious, ambivalent, vicious, sarcastic, cynical or dismissive.

Tone of voice is a powerful means of communication both for the person who is communicating and for the person at the receiving end of the non-verbal message. In terms of the speaker, when psychological safety is present, tone of voice offers a powerful window into his or her own interior world. In owning both aspects of voice tone, the speaker is given the opportunity to check the source of the tone, and when it is protective in nature and expressing particular emergency feelings such as anger, sadness or fear it provides the opportunity to enhance one's inner stronghold of Self.

For example, if you notice your tone of voice is frequently cross, you may discover the intention to convey anger was an attempt to get another person – adult or child – to take responsibility for some unmet need of yours, rather than you yourself taking ownership of it. This happened to a teacher friend of mine who found that each day he went home from teaching school, feeling stressed and tired, he was cross with his five-year-old son with whom the relationship had sadly deteriorated. In experiencing psychological safety, he realised he was not looking after himself and that it was this neglect he was projecting on to his unsuspecting, baffled and hurt son.

When psychological safety is present, the person who is the target of another's tone of voice has an opportunity to examine his or her present level of protectiveness. When a person personalises the other's tone of voice – for example, reading the other's tone of voice as disrespectful of him or her – then enmeshment is present. The query for the person is "How is it that in the face of the threatening tone of voice that I did not stay separate, hold on to my own sense of worthiness of respect and say 'I'm not at all clear on what your tone of voice is communicating'?" Whether it is a non-verbal or verbal communication, the message coming from the other is totally about the person sending the message and says *nothing* about the receiver. When you safeguardingly receive it as being about you, if and when you find psychological safety, it now becomes an opportunity to work on your own relationship with yourself – conscious genius.

Chapter Eight:
The Difference Between Safety and Safeguarding

- Psychological Safety to Differ
- Screen Self – Real Self
- Enmeshment – Separateness
- Cognition – Emotion
- Content – Context
- Expectation – Request
- Change – Emergence
- Teaching – Learning

Psychological safety to differ

The word differentiation contains three words and concepts that are essential to psychological safety teaching and learning and to psychological safety managing and leading: differ, different and differentiate.

As a parent or teacher or manager or leader, do you consciously dare to differ, to question, to challenge, or do you unconsciously conform or rebel in the face of difference? *Difference is the source of creativity*. When the differences between us are acknowledged, each holds to his or her own beliefs, values, methods and also shows interest in the different ways of the other. There is no attempt to impose and there is real curiosity in examining where the other person is at and vice versa. In the conversation that develops, each may learn something from the other that deepens his or her stance and when each accepts the difference between them, then, at least, there has been mutual learning that there can be differences without conflict. When one person categorically disagrees with the other person's point of view, then there is no room for learning and creativity as the protective aggressive message is 'I'm right and you're wrong'. It is in this way that disagreement becomes a source of conflict and intransigence, whereas embracing difference becomes a source of psychological safety, creativity, development and tolerance.

It reminds me of a time when I was doing a day workshop with a primary school staff group. I presented the idea that attainment is always present in a child's efforts to learn and the response to a child's classwork or homework needs to focus on identifying what attainments are present and not on performance. When a teacher focuses on performance, the answer is either right or wrong and, when wrong, this response is generally done with a red pen, adding to the child's pain of failure or not feeling good enough.

Take the example where a child is asked to spell a particular word – let us say calendar. When the child's attempt is incorrect, the teacher who marks performance will put a red x next to the word; the teacher who marks attainment will give a √ for effort and several √s for each letter correctly placed. For example, with an attainment response, the child who spells calendar as *calender* will get seven

√s showing an attainment of seven correct out of eight letters – wow! Such a response acknowledges all that the child has attained and the next step of learning how to complete the spelling of the word. Marking attainment maintains a child's love of learning; performance-driven education can dry up motivation or increase the pressure to conform. In both cases the joy of learning may be extinguished. Performance-driven education would mark the child's spelling effort as follows: calender x. No matter what the level of education, the fact is that performance anxiety is epidemic.

Back to the story. Some time after the workshop, one of the teachers approached me and revealed "I've always marked children's school and homework in the way you demonstrated." I responded, adding "And how is it that you did not broadcast your wonderful idea?" The teacher replied "Ah, they (parents and teachers) would only see me as a softie." The fear of judgment and criticism results in so many creations not seeing the light of day. Daring to differ means staying open to new ideas and methods of teaching and actively exploring new possibilities all the time. When it is frightening to differ then the unconscious psychological safeguarding response is to batten down the hatches and be conformist or become very aggressive when somebody sees and does things differently from you – this can be a colleague, a school principal, a student or a parent, or even a visiting lecturer!

Each child is different, not only in his or her unique presence but also each child has a different story. The story contains the environments in which the child lives daily, most especially it contains the child's different responses to the external events in his or her life, and these can be of a psychological safeguarding or psychological safety nature. Oliver James, in his book *Not in Your Genes* is very definite in his belief that the first three years of a child's life are critical to wellbeing and can be the basis of a difficult or exciting life. By the time the child comes to pre-school or primary school, his or her level of trust is well established. If the child has encountered considerable trauma arising from the threatening/safeguarding behaviours of parents and child-minders, he or she will wisely have created not only unconscious psychological safeguards to reduce threats but also substitute ways of gaining attention.

There is no substitute for the real thing, which is unconditional love of the child's person and unrepeatable presence. But when this is not present children are *heroic* at finding alternative ways of getting attention – by being pleasing, shy, ill, disruptive, having temper tantrums, being the 'best', withdrawing from contact, hurting themselves, and multiple other ways. When children are unconditionally held they present as secure, confident, cooperative and wonderfully curious.

Naturally, what is true of the child is also true of the teacher (or parent or manager or leader); each is different and unique and also has a story that is different from any other person. As for the child, when the adult in question has a solid interiority, she or he is everybody's favourite adult because she or he is operating consciously and poses no threat to a child's presence and she or he will manage 'difficult' behaviours with kindness, patience and understanding. For example, if a teacher with a solid interiority needs extra help and support to manage some children's behaviours, there will be no hesitancy in seeking it out. She or he knows too that each child has a different teacher and that the relationship with each is unique, and is conscious that each teacher has a different student and that the relationship that emerges between them is a unique co-creation.

When a teacher unconsciously lives life from the outside-in and is, for example, dependent on the perception of others, is performance driven, irritable, impatient, perfectionist, insecure, uncertain, dominating, impersonal, then, unwittingly, great threats are posed to children's wellbeing and especially to those children who already have been traumatised. Unless these kinds of psychological safeguards are kindly detected by a colleague or school principal as signalling a cry for help, then, sadly, for that teacher and the students there is no light at the end of the tunnel. (This is true also for managers and leaders.)

A frequent protective response from teachers is "I treat all the children the same." The source of this attitude is, undoubtedly, that these teachers do not consciously see their own uniqueness. The consequence is that the students are depersonalised. The only resolution of this sad scenario is where these teachers are helped and supported to experience awe of their own unique presence and that of each student.

The foregoing has emphasised seeing how every teacher, parent and student (and leader and manager) is different:

- Individuality (there's no one like you)
- Story (social connection) – the influence of early relationships on the student, parent and teacher, and manager and leader
- Interiority (psychic connection) – the degree to which the teacher, parent and student, and leader and manager is connected (psychological safety) or disconnected (psychological safeguarding) from Self
- Passions – each student, parent and teacher, and leader and manager develops passions that are individual and deserve to be acknowledged and nurtured
- Priorities – in a classroom, the student's priorities may differ radically from that of the teacher due to family influences outside of the school, as will those of a parent, teacher, manager and leader

When psychological safety is present the pre-school and primary school curriculum will prioritise the unmet needs of the child, and create ways of meeting these needs:

- *Physical:* Experiences of being starved, poorly fed, overfed, slapping, pushing, being punched, kicked, hit and shouted at. The child's physical needs are to be nurtured with good food, his/her tastes taken into consideration, be hugged, requested to cooperate and experience no threats to his/her physical wellbeing.

- *Emotional:* For example, feeling unloved, being compared, full of fears, emotionally withdrawn, temper outbursts. The child's emotional needs are unconditional love and holding of all expressions of feelings – welfare (signalling wellbeing) and emergency (signalling trauma).

- *Social:* Connection to one or both parents (often different) being of an overbelonging (smothering, spoilt) nature, underbelonging (unpredictable and inconsistent expressions of love and active involvement) and no belonging (no connection whatsoever). The child requires that his/her presence and absence always matter.

- *Symbiotic belonging:* In this kind of belonging individuality of any kind is not tolerated – the family moves as one. Children need unconditional and individualised connection.

- *Sexual:* Punishment of a child's natural curiosity or of self-stimulation, early sexualising of the child, sexual violations. Where psychological safety is present, there is accompanying of the child's emerging sexuality – no threats and ways found to resolve adverse sexual experiences.

- *Intellectual:* Overemphasis or underemphasis of the child's intellectual development, pressure to perform, punishment of mistakes, tying of affection to accomplishments, poor nurturing of natural curiosity and risk-taking. Where psychological safety is present there is an accompaniment of the child's eagerness to learn and love of learning – no pressure, just pleasure.

- *Behavioural:* The child is deprived of opportunities to do things for Self, no nurturing of the toddler's most common demand "I do, I do." The child's efforts to do for Self are met with spoiling, irritability, impatience, criticism, comparisons or put-downs, such that the child stops trying or attempts to get it perfect. The parent and teacher who bring psychological safety to children will consistently encourage the child's ability to do for Self – obviously age-related.

- *Creative:* The capacity to be creative is in our nature but pressures to conform influence the nature of the conscious emergence of creativity. Similarly, the message to do what is expected inevitably sends creativity underground – the creativity of this response is rarely appreciated. Conscious belief in the amazing unique creativity that each possesses, and adults doing themselves what they would like the child to do, is what truly nurtures conscious creativity.

The third consideration is how well do school staff and managers and leaders *differentiate* between the following two sets of concepts:

Unconsciousness	Consciousness
Behaviour	Person
Knowledge	Intelligence
Screen Self	Real Self
Enmeshment	Separateness
Dependence	Independence

Fearfulness	Fearlessness
Protectors	Boundaries
Conditional	Unconditional
Depression	Expression
Outside-in	Inside-out
Cognition	Emotion
Technique	Relationship
Content	Context
Expectation	Request
Judgment	Understanding
Imposition	Accompanying
Failure	Attainment
Success	Achievement
Pressure	Encouragement
Change	Emergence
Teaching	Learning
Literal	Symbolic
Talking to/at	Talking with
Surviving	Thriving

Psychological safety is the path to differentiation. When you operate primarily from the left-hand column of the above listed dualities, you have cleverly become blinkered, and depending on the amount that you have needed to blind yourself to, you will come to a place of realising the two sides of the outlined dimensions only when there is considerable psychological safety from another who is in that place of differentiation. This person sees both sides of the coin, and even though he or she will mainly relate to Self, others and the world in the ways named in the right-hand column, he or she will appreciate the creativity and wisdom of those who, out of unconscious psychological safeguarding, had to forsake many aspects of the depth and breadth of being consciously human. Some of the dualities listed have already been considered; those not previously considered are discussed below.

Screen Self — Real Self

The screen is the psychological safeguarding walls behind which you hide. This screen is your way of surviving the screen behaviours of others. When you are a child, due to your dependence on parents and other key adults in your life, the screen has to be such that you somehow or other found the means to stay enmeshed with these adult figures because the devil you know is better than the devil you do not know! Of course, the threats to your wellbeing are not reserved for your earlier years, but can even intensify in the adult settings in which you live, learn, play, pray and work. The reason for this is that all adults suffer in their early years — on a continuum of low to very intense — and nobody escapes in our fearful relationships where person is continually confused with behaviour.

The adult who primarily lives life from a screen place clearly does not differentiate between Screen Self and Real Self; indeed, he or she may be quite dismissive and even aggressive around this concept of Self. But then such a reaction (anagram of creation) makes total sense when you realise that to accept that there is a Real Self would mean daring to risk again being real and authentic – a dangerous possibility, given all the abandonments up to this time; wiser to stay hidden and to test the waters several times before a tentative emergence. Individuals who can differentiate between the two selves have found the psychological safety to be conscious and to now act from a real place – no hiding – and manifest their individuality and apply their intelligence and creativity to deepening expression of Self, with others and the world. It is not that they do not at times slip back into screen behaviour, but at least they are more likely to detect that shift and take ownership of it and return to the truth of who they are and what they wish to say or do in the here-and-now.

Enmeshment – Separateness

Each of us is an island and that guardianship of that aloneness (all-one-ness) is an essential aspect of a conscious relationship between any two people: parent-child, teacher-student, husband-wife, friend-friend, lover-lover, or employer-employee. It is individuals and not systems who determine the quality of an environment; it is only through individuals that the ethos of a couple relationship, family, classroom, school, community, workplace, church or country can there be a psychological safety that is inclusive or dark and divisive. Adults who have remained enmeshed with family of origin, or live in enmeshed marriages, or are enmeshed with how they are perceived by others, or with role performance, are necessarily in deeply unconscious psychological safeguarding places and, as a result, will unconsciously create environments that are threatening in nature.

Separateness is the basis for togetherness in all relationships, whereby you consciously inhabit your own individuality, are independent and respond with awe to the unique presence of the other and nurture, support and encourage their independence from the moment of birth to death. Parents who live their lives through their children are enmeshed and it is dangerous for their children to oppose what is being projected on to them. Equally, a parent who lives her life for her child unwittingly prevents that child from living his or her own life and becoming separate. Those parents who are not there for their children, because there was not psychological safety for them to be there for themselves, do not mirror their children's individuality and age-related ability to take charge of their own lives. There is little hope for these children unless parents are provided with the psychological safety to come into consciousness of their true and amazing nature.

Similarly, for teachers, their level of enmeshment with key figures in their lives and with work will largely determine the classroom environment. If it is essential for parents to become separate, it is equally vital for teachers to do so. Indeed, it is an urgent development for all adults who have managerial or leadership roles where people work, train, play, heal and pray to become consciously separate. It is a real paradox that the more separate you are in your relationship with another – child, spouse, colleague, school principal, workplace leader, manager – the deeper and closer is the relationship. In such a relationship you bring your fullness to another and see the fullness of the other (even though they may not be conscious of it). In being separate, your boundary around the island of your Self will not allow any invasions (enmeshments) to that precious interiority. Finally, when you realise your separateness and clearly differentiate it from enmeshment, you will be conscious that enmeshment has been a necessary psychological safeguard in the face of the protectors of others and you will feel compassion for yourself and for them.

Cognition – Emotion

There has been and continues to be a belief that changing an adult's or a child's way of thinking is what is required when either presents with troubling or troubled behaviour. In spite of the evidence to the contrary – that altering thoughts changes nothing (Schore, 2012) – there persists a movement to offer CBT (cognitive behaviour therapy) or its more recent development DBT (dialectical behaviour therapy) which incorporates aspects of the Mindfulness approach to human suffering. In regard to the latter, whilst I very much encourage and practise meditation myself, I do not want to distract from what is present emotionally or cognitively or physically or socially because that is precisely where the person needs to be! When a person tells me "I feel nothing for myself" I do not want to divert him to being present to the chair on which he is sitting or to the ambience of the room; I want to stay with his alarming message and explore with him *how* that feels, *how* did he come to see himself as 'nothing', and begin to explore how unconsciously he has psychologically safeguarded himself in hiding his true Self behind the screen of feeling nothing for himself. His line "I feel nothing for myself" points me in the direction of his story and how he experienced being nothing in the eyes of one or both parents – an absolutely terrifying experience.

If I respond to his cognition "I feel nothing for myself" with "That is a very negative and irrational thing to say about yourself" there is an immediate criticism of his behaviour and this response on my part will most likely exacerbate his pain – one more person who does not love him for himself and understand him, and fails to show belief in his creativity. Seeing the deeper emotional message, having a sense and a desire to know the story behind the 'depressing' (all the put-downs) experiences and developing a sense of awe of his presence and how he has heroically survived is what is urgently required. Thoughts then are neither 'positive' nor 'negative' but creative pathways into what lies hidden. When you can hold cognitions in that way and seek the underlying emotion, then you are cleverly differentiating between cognition and emotion and holding each as co-partners in the quest to conscious seeing and expression of Self.

Content – Context

There is a shift occurring in psychosocial therapies, and in psychiatry, towards examining not just the content of a child's or adult's distress but also the context in which that distress has occurred and/or is still happening. On the basis of the content of the physical and psychosocial symptoms with which they present, many children and adults have been labelled by a health professional employing a checklist of 'abnormal behaviours' and, literally, ticking the boxes. No examination of story (context) is carried out or, if it is, it is not included as an essential part of the therapeutic assessment and intervention required. When looking at context (the external environments, past and present) the threats that the child or adult encountered are certainly noted, but what is still missing is an even more important consideration of the internal environment created in response to the threatening external environment – the unconscious hero's journey.

There is a growing acceptance that as a child the unconsciously formed psychological safeguards were adaptive solutions to the perceived threats, but these protectors are labelled as psychiatric disorders or psychological dysfunctions in adulthood. Ironically, the epidemic labelling of children does not take into consideration the adaptive and creative nature of their psychological safeguards. When content (presenting safeguards) and context (both external and internal environments) are differentiated, then all that is past and present is held, be it nurturing or troubling, and consciousness is present – in parent, teacher, or psychosocial practitioner, or healthcare provider – to respond meaningfully to another, whether child or adult.

When you are in an unconscious psychological safeguarded place and label and judge another's challenging behaviours as bad, insane, irrational, dysfunctional, disordered, inappropriate, negative, disturbed, then you yourself are crying out for psychological safety to come into consciousness of your present stance; you are certainly not in the psychological safety place to respond therapeutically to the traumatised child or adult. Whether it is the home, the classroom, the school, the community or the workplace, consciousness of the impact of these environments on both children and adults can be present only when there is clear differentiation between content and context, and of the contribution of both to the level of wellbeing for all. What will also be present is consciousness of the power and creativity of the person's internal and unconscious safeguarding responses to the threats experienced (the hidden content).

Expectation – Request

Enrolling the cooperation of children in homes and classrooms, and of adults in various social and work settings, is an important part of creating conscious empowering and equal relationship with them. Accompanying children and adults where they are at – they never cease to communicate – and discovering their needs through whatever behaviours are presenting deepens contact. When adults have needs of children, and a realisation is present that those needs are of, belong to and are for the adult – parent or teacher – then expectation will be differentiated from request. When parents or teachers make a request of a child, ownership of their own need is actively present, and they kindly invite the cooperation of the child and accept that the child may or may not be in a place to accede to the expressed need.

When a child is heedless or stubbornly says "No", separateness is essential and the enquiry "How is it that you're not heeding what I'm saying?" or "How is it that you are saying 'no' to what I'm requesting?" Recall too that tone of voice needs to be noted since a crossly expressed need severs the unconditional relationship with the child and the child's non-cooperation can be more to do with the experience of rejection than with a particular hidden need of the child. When adults have an expectation that the child 'should' meet their needs, they are unconsciously passing on responsibility for their needs to the child and, inevitably, this will lead to an enmeshed relationship.

Unmet expectations lead to feelings of disappointment and resentment and create distance in the relationships. The realisation is enlightening that the source of the disappointment and resentment always lies within the person who expressed the need; these feelings tugging at her or his consciousness that she or he is not operating from an inner psychological safety place of separateness and independence and is now being invited to do just that. The disappointment calls for an appointment with Self and the resentment for an ownership of one's own needs.

When having expectations of others arises, this is an opportunity, when there is psychological safety, to examine their source and to come to a place of ownership of them. Incidentally, when a child or adult is continually uncooperative, this is an indication that there are deeper issues involved that far exceed the expressed unmet need. Continuing to make requests such as "I would really like to know how it is that any time I express a need, I get a 'no'" may create the psychological safety for the other person to reveal the sources of uncooperativeness.

Change – Emergence

I say to all individuals, young and old, who come to me for what they see as needing to change: "I would not want to change a hair on your head!" If I say to a person that I will help them to change, there is an implicit criticism that where you are now is wrong and together we need to make it right. What an odd place from which to start therapy! *Where you are right now is where you need to be.* All that you have hidden about your real Self was wisely done and all the safeguarding ways you found to get attention or experience a substitute high, arising from love being "tortured by its own hunger and thirst" (Kahlil Gibran) were and are clever psychological creations. Nothing needs changing and the work of therapy is to create a relationship with you where you will begin to experience the psychological safety to *emerge* from hiding and, slowly but surely, and just as creatively as you have found unconscious ways to hide, you will create conscious and real ways to experience your fullness, even in a world full of danger. The parent and teacher who bring psychological safety to children and adults differentiate very clearly between change and emergence, and know that believing in the need for change represents a call to reflection on where they are in themselves and the realisation that it is all about emergence that happens when psychological safety is offered.

Teaching – Learning

Conscious teachers know that it is their responsibility to teach and to bring their passion for their subjects to the students. They know too that learning belongs to the child and that any confusion between the teacher's teaching and the child's learning will interrupt the teacher-child relationship and will lead to enmeshment of the evaluation of teaching with the child's learning outcomes. As for everything else, teaching is of the teacher, belongs to the teacher and is for the teacher. Similarly, learning is of the student, belongs to the student and is for the student.

I recall being asked to talk to a student who had four times failed her entrance examination to a particular university faculty, in spite of her showing remarkable promise in the lecture hall. The lecturers were puzzled by her repeated failure and were questioning their own teaching ability. My educated guess was that there were some hidden emotional issues that the repeated failures were attempting to draw attention to, something she dared not voice directly. It had become an urgent matter as she had only one chance left to progress into faculty. When I met her, I was taken by her academic knowledge levels and knew quickly there was a hidden failure that needed to come to the surface so that the examination failures could be resolved.

As our contact deepened, she revealed to me that she was terrified of letting her father down and that when she sat the examination this fear overwhelmed her, resulting in her not remembering all that she knew. Wise fear! I explored with her the source of her fear. She told me that her father had always wanted one of his children to go to university, but none of them had done so – wise avoidance! She was the youngest and the last hope for her father – hence the immense pressure. We explored the truth that she was here to live her own life – not her father's life – and she would (unconsciously) be failing herself if she continued to try to please him. Yes, she loved her father, but love is not about conformity but about independence and separateness. She did pass the final test, but this time her effort was for herself, not for her father.

For the sake of the teachers, the students and the ethos of the school, the differentiation between teaching and learning is vital to the emotional wellbeing of all concerned and, indeed, the educational progress of the students. Teachers who enmesh teaching with learning are unconsciously putting their needs for recognition and success on the shoulders of students, which will necessitate the students finding some clever way to reduce the threat arising from the teacher's projection on to them – for example, going for the average, thereby lowering the teacher's expectations, competing for the teacher's attention by being the 'best student', being disruptive in class so that the teacher's attention is switched to managing discipline rather than high academic expectations.

The psychological safety teacher keeps the two worlds separate – teaching and learning – and whilst she or he is interested in the child's present learning potential, nevertheless the teacher knows that how the child is learning right now speaks volumes about the child's current motivation to learn and, very often, adverse family circumstances. The latter are generally a function of parents' interest in the child's educational development and, not infrequently, family and marital conflict, but can also reflect unconscious psychological safeguarding responses to where the teacher is at in terms of teaching and learning.

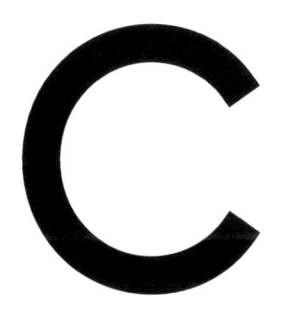

Chapter Nine:
Psychological Safety Teaching, Leadership and Management

- Education and Occupation as Co-Creations
- Inspiring Children and Employees
- Creating Psychological Safety for Parents, Teachers, Leaders and Managers
- Parents, Teachers, Leaders and Managers Realising their Own Genius and Talents
- The Presence of Enduring Unconditional Love
- No Affection to be Attached to Achievement
- Belief is Everything!
- Engage in and Encourage Practice and Persistence
- Embrace Failure and Success as Opportunities
- Model and Support Originality

Education and occupation as co-creations

In the teaching and learning of any subject, both teacher and student come to the classroom not with clean psychic slates from which the teacher can passionately and freely educate and the student can eagerly and excitedly learn without any interruptions to that wonderful experience. As seen in earlier chapters, each teacher and each student has a unique story and the nature of that inner and outer story will determine how the teacher teaches, how the student learns, and how each responds to the other. Equally, in the leadership and management of any organisation, leaders and managers do not come to the organisation with clean psychic slates from which they can freely lead and manage and employees can eagerly and excitedly work without any interruptions to that productive experience.

The second consideration is that most of the ways teachers and students and leaders/managers and employees act and interact – emotional, social, sexual, intellectual, creative, behavioural and physical – are unconsciously created and unless what lies hidden becomes conscious, no inner alignment with Self or outer alignment in the person-to-person contact between teacher and student and leader/manager and employee and their multiple needs of each other is likely. Indeed, the most powerful eclipsing of classroom and workplace possibilities arises from either a partial or a total eclipse of the Self of the teacher or student or both and of the leader/manager or employee or both.

Creating a climate of emotional, intellectual, physical and social safety in classrooms and workplaces is essential for teacher and student and leader/manager and employee to bring to light and resolve hidden inner and outer conflicts so that unconditional regard is mutual or, at least, the teacher or leader/manager occupies a solid interiority and consequently can empathically stay separate from a student's or employee's challenging responses and support resolution of same and, where necessary, to avail of a conscious relationship practitioner.

Inspiring children and employees

In the same way that teaching and leadership/management matter enormously in educationally inspiring a child and occupationally inspiring an employee so too does parenting. As already discussed, parents are the first educators and there is major evidence to show how the first three years of a child's life – before the child ever sees a teacher or, later on, a leader/manager – will determine how much the child will have retained love of learning and eagerness to learn.

In the beginning, the infant and toddler exhibit the following qualities and behaviours:

- Reliance
- Genius
- Natural curiosity
- Love of learning
- Endless energy
- Risk-taking
- Fearlessness
- Not bothered by failure
- Aliveness
- Expansiveness
- Not bothered by success
- Spontaneity
- Eagerness

- 'I do, I do' phenomenon
- Confidence

There is much that parents can do to support and encourage their children to achieve but they can do this only to the extent that they have retained or redeemed some or all of the natural qualities listed above. Schools could be the ideal centres for parents of pre-school children to examine in a psychological safety environment where they are in terms of their own sense of Self, in terms of the degree to which they consciously express their genius and love of learning, and in terms of the fears and hurts around education that may unconsciously be influencing how they are in themselves and how they are around their children. Such a service would be of considerable benefit to the parents, to their children and, most especially, for the future teachers of these pre-school children. If what is hidden in parents and in their pre-school children is revealed and resolved, then teachers can get down to the business of what they are trained to do – teaching. Equally, leaders/managers can get down to the business of what they are trained to do – leading/managing.

The serious matter of inspiring children in homes, classrooms and adults in workplaces involves:

- Creating psychological safety for parents, teachers, leaders and managers
- Parents, teachers, leaders and managers realising their own genius and talents
- The presence of enduring unconditional love
- No affection to be attached to achievements
- Belief is everything!
- Engage in and encourage practice and persistence

- Embrace failure and success as opportunities
- Model and support originality

Creating psychological safety for parents, teachers, leaders and managers

There is nobody who has not experienced interruptions to their presence and to the expression of natural curiosity, eagerness to learn, emotional expression, expression of needs, fearlessness, risk-taking and spontaneity. The reality is that for most adults fear dominates their lives and leads them to unconsciously creating powerful ways of reducing all the threats encountered in the past and now in the present. Fear of what others think, of not being good enough, of failure, of success, of criticism, of judgment, of being laughed at, demeaned, lessened, dismissed, compared and humiliated are some typical examples. What is often not appreciated is that threats are not confined to the family environment; indeed, threats can multiply when children go to child-minders, pre-school, primary and second-level schools, and later on into higher education and the workplace.

The higher the number of threats, the higher the number of protectors created, until a time comes when a parent or teacher or leader or manager finds the psychological safety from another who occupies a solid interiority and is largely fearless. Certainly, if in your younger years you experienced unconditional holding, nurturance, patience, kindness, understanding, encouragement, belief in you and were accompanied by your parents who were emotionally attuned to your inner world, then you will have the benefit of parents who will champion you when you encounter threats in social and educational environments beyond the home. Your parents are your heroes and you also will become a conscious hero for yourself.

It is essential that psychological safety opportunities be made available to parents and teachers and leaders and managers to examine their lives so that their lived lives can be an inspiration to their young or older charges. Carl Jung (in Hollis 2005) expressed this poignantly: "What usually has the strongest psychic effect on children is the life which the parents have not lived." My experience is that this can also be true for the psychic effects that teachers have on children and leaders and managers have on employees. Parents and teachers and leaders and managers (and indeed all professionals) deserve the opportunities to explore their inner worlds and bring to consciousness all that they dare not speak or do openly. This service needs to be offered by practitioners who have examined and continue to examine their own inner worlds so that they largely come to inhabiting a solid interiority.

Parents, teachers, leaders and managers realising their own genius and talents

At presentations on many topics all over the world, a question I often ask is: "How many of you here can put up your hand and assert 'I know I am a genius'?" Of all the thousands asked this question, there have been only around 10 affirmative replies. It is then not surprising that there are so few children who have any conscious sense of their genius. I cringe at the time when I was teaching and had no sense of my own genius and even less of the genius of the students. The birthright of each parent and teacher and leader/manager, no matter what age, to come into consciousness of their power beyond measure is crucial, not only for their sense of overall wellbeing but also for that of those in their care.

At one particular conference, a tearful looking participant approached me, telling me that though she was a qualified and practising teacher she had what she described as 'a call' to train in clinical psychology. But she felt that others, particularly her parents and colleagues, would be critical of her leaving a good pensionable job. This young woman was 25 years of age. I told her my own story of seven years in a monastery and subsequent training in primary and second-level teaching, and then my decision, at age 30, in spite of poor financial resources, to return to university and study psychology and later clinical psychology full time over a period of eight years. I encouraged her to follow her passion as staying with a profession that was not inspirational for her would result in her life not being lived. She said "You're my hero" to which I replied "And what an opportunity to be a conscious heroine for yourself."

Every parent and teacher and leader and manager deserves to find a conscious hero who will create the psychological safety for them to:

- Find what they love to do
- Be conscious that genius is always present – either in screen or real expression
- Be their own champion in their pursuit of their passions
- See the attainment and opportunity in every failure and mistake (it is regrettable that few parents and teachers and leaders and managers turn failure into opportunity but instead operate to make failure a source of humiliation and embarrassment and consequently extinguish passion)
- Commit to the pursuit of excellence but not confuse Self with excellence
- Be conscious that there is no substitute for their unique presence
- Be assured that there is no age of impossibility
- Be conscious that talent is a quiet step-by-step incremental development over time

- Enjoy the small accomplishments as the jigsaw pieces come together to eventually complete the full picture (knowledge, skills and talent are always the result of consistent and persistent and original practice)
- Identify endless external resources
- Come to know they are heroes
- Find a teacher or leader/manager who inspires (there are few of us who were lucky enough to have had at least one teacher who inspired, believed in us, encouraged, supported, emphasised attainments and exhibited endless faith in us and patience. Those individuals who were fortunate to have had such a teacher tend to wax lyrical on what a difference that teacher made. Those who had teachers who unwittingly failed to inspire can have a lot of bitter memories of their school days)

The above realisations equally apply to leaders and managers in different organisational worlds.

It is now clear that genius is always present as is achievement – either in screen (unconscious) or real (conscious) way. The path is in each discovering the psychological safety to find his or her own passion, maintaining determination, using the limitless resources available and knowing that achievement is not age-related, and that creativity is possible to the time of death. It is also clear that parenting and teaching and leading and managing do powerfully matter. There is so much that parents and teachers and leaders and managers can do to support and encourage their charges to thrive. But, as seen, parents and teachers cannot provide for children what they are not doing for themselves; neither can leaders and managers provide for employees what they are not doing for themselves. Hence the emphasis on parents and teachers and leaders and managers *first* – otherwise, the chances of children not closing down and repressing the wonders of their nature are very slim indeed or employees daring to come out from behind their safeguarding walls.

The presence of enduring unconditional love

Unconditional love is the deepest longing not only of every child but also of every adult, and there is no greater threat to a person's wellbeing when it is not persistently present. Of course, all parents and teachers can at times be conditional, but once they quickly make up with the child and acknowledge to themselves and to the child, in an age-related fashion, that they had lapsed in the unconditional love of themselves, children recover their sense of security. The truth is that the depth and extent of the unconditional love that a parent or teacher or leader or manager has for Self is what they can show the child or employee – the child or employee is you! When parents and teachers and leaders and managers had to create a thousand masks to hide their real Selves, no matter how well-intentioned they are, they cannot give a child or employee what they do not consciously feel for themselves and did not receive when they were children.

Unconditional love is the awe-response to the individual presence of the child and adult and no challenging behaviour on the child's or adult's part will rock the ship of unconditionality. Once a man approached me following a talk on 'The Deepest Longing' and said "I just don't get this unconditional bit." I asked what would evoke unconditional love in him for his child; his answer spoke volumes: "If the child smiled at me." My response was "So your son is going to have to smile up at you for the rest of his days in order to get affection from you." The man walked away still muttering that he "did not get it" but returned shortly with his wife declaring that he "had got it" and telling me about their troubled teenager who was screaming out for unconditional holding.

The realisation was not only critical for his son but also for himself and for his wife who had passively put up with his grumpiness for many years. If irritability tells a story so too does the maintenance of silence. Parents and teachers and leaders and managers who have the support to do their conscious utmost in their relationship with themselves and their charges do not jeopardise this essential connection over any piece of behaviour – whether of a challenging or a pleasing nature. Love is for the person, not behaviour, and love is not to be connected to learning or withdrawn when failure occurs.

No affection to be attached to achievement

When parents and teachers or leaders and managers unconsciously attach affection and recognition to achievement, they seriously disrupt not only the child's and employee's sense of his or her separate and unrepeatable Self but also their natural eagerness to learn and explore. The child will secretly and wisely come to believe that in order to be loved he or she needs to be exceptional in some way or another. The unconscious genius formation of an addiction to pleasing parents and teachers occurs and also the addiction to success. The word addiction *speaks loudly* of the serious interruptions experienced. Indeed, depending on the intensity, frequency and endurance of tying affection to achievement, children can become emotionally threatened and subsequently devastated when parents in particular, but also teachers, go cold when they do not live up to what is expected.

I recall a mother contacting me about her daughter who was studying medicine at university. On the phone, the mother told me how her daughter had got the highest results in the country in the second-level Leaving Certificate examination and had no difficulty in securing a university place for medical training. But the mother went on to say her daughter had recently failed an oral examination and had taken to her bed, was deeply depressed and suicidal and was refusing to return to university. When the mother asked if I could help her daughter, I replied that I could help her not to confuse her sense of Self with an examination result. To which the mother responded "And, Doctor, how soon will you have my daughter back at university?" I mistakenly replied "I can certainly support your daughter to become fearless around achievements but her decision to return to university I would need to leave entirely to herself." The mother slammed down the phone and my learning was that the mother needed more unconditional holding than the daughter!

An important question here is: if affection is not to be tied to achievement, what response then does a parent or teacher or leader or manager give to an achievement? Achievement is a natural reward in itself; there is little to match the satisfaction that spontaneously arises when you complete another step along the unending road of achievement. Certainly, parents and teachers or leaders and managers can focus on their own and on the child's emotional response to an achievement and hold to the reality that *inner satisfaction* is integral to learning and outer affection and praise jeopardise that natural experience. The enquiry that best supports children and adults when they achieve is "I'd like to hear how you feel about what you have accomplished" – there is no imposition here.

Equally, it is supportive to send an 'I-message': "I'm impressed by your work but it is how you feel about it that really matters." Usually, when affection and praise are attached to an achievement it is done through a 'you-message' – "you're a great boy" or "you've done us proud" or "you're the best" or "you're a great worker" or "you're an inspiration to us all". An 'I-message' expresses something about the inner experience of the parent or teacher or leader or manager and is of, belongs to and is for the parent or teacher or leader or manager. It lets the child or adult know something about the other but it is not about the child or employee. Only the child or employee can tell what his or her inner experience is like.

The 'you' communication is an unconscious projection on to the child's or employee's behaviour and arises from a fearful place within the adult. For example, "you're a wonderful child" or "you're so clever" often project the parent's or the teacher's or leader's or manager's repressed need to see their own wonder or cleverness. The adult who has a solid interiority and speaks from a real genius place when communicating with a child or other adult will say "I love the wonder of you" and "I enjoy the ways you manifest your cleverness" – no imposition and a pure accompaniment with what is true of the child and of the adult.

When during therapy I communicate to a person that "I am in awe of your presence", the client may respond "I have no such feeling for myself." My response is that I hear that and, given your horrific story that has emerged, I understand it and see how psychologically safeguarding it was for you to bury your presence behind the screen of having no feeling for yourself. What a wonderful protection hating yourself is, since it means you no longer put yourself out there to be rejected again. When individuals begin to trust the expressed deep love and genuine regard for them, they will gradually and wisely emerge from behind the screen to a real genius place. Trust builds slowly when the most important adults in your life – parents, siblings and teachers – were and still are not in a place to unconditionally love you and mirror your genius from consciousness of their own lovability and genius.

Belief is everything!

The phrase 'belief is everything' came from a young man in his late teens who came to see me for help. So many young people smartly screen belief in themselves, arising from the fact that neither their parents nor teachers possessed belief in themselves, due to their childhood experiences and experiences in later life – "the endless repetition of the mistake" as described by D. H. Lawrence (1885-1930) in his poem called *Healing*.

It has been demonstrated that talent is not inherent or inborn but trained and educated, and with exceptional teaching and persistence any child, or adult, can attain conscious achievements. When parents and teachers or leaders/managers realise their own limitless potential, they can mirror this for children and employees and have the determination for themselves and for the children and employees to muster whatever resources are needed for each to continue to nurture their own individual potential. Expression of belief in each child and adult, from the belief in Self, through modelling and the 'I-message', as well as persistent involvement, aids this vital process. A reminder is warranted here that conscious achievements are not in any way less ingenious as unconscious achievements.

Engage in and encourage practice and persistence

Above all else, adults exhibiting curiosity and attending to the child's natural curiosity are what maintain an eagerness to learn. Practice and persistence considerably support learning and, indeed, are what determine the difference between average and high achievement. What is important here is that you ask children or adults to do only what you are doing yourself in the here-and-now and in the future. Recall that in every learning effort there is always an attainment and focus on that reality. Conscious psychological safety adults provide plenty of opportunities for practice for themselves and children and employees, and demonstrate how well they stay with a task and how they cope with and ease frustration when it arises. Examples here are talking about their frustration, taking a break, giving themselves a treat – whatever soothes! These adults model and reassure others that staying with a task always reaps the natural rewards that come with accomplishments. They are wary of the temptation to give external rewards because when these cease so does persistence.

Embrace failure and success as opportunities

Those who embrace failure and success as co-partners on the road to learning thrive. They see attainment in each failure and work out from that stable base and view success as the stepping stone to further learning. The joy is in the wonderful rotation of failure and success on the never-ending open doors they provide for ongoing learning. Indeed, the only true failure is to give up or to unconsciously sell yourself or the child or adult short. But when this is the case there is an opportunity for that adult to reflect on his or her own story.

There can be an unconscious protective counterproductive tendency on the part of parents and teachers and leaders and managers to make things easier for children or employees or to do the task for them. What children and employees require are adults to present, monitor and modulate challenges for them and maintain their belief in them. Patience is essential and when a child/adult struggles with understanding a concept or mastering a skill, the psychological safety adult is wary of engaging in what has happened to many children and adults – a belief that they are incapable of progressing. The fact is that when an adult believes such of the child and other adult, it is about themselves and their psychological safeguarding belief that they do not have the belief to persist in the teaching of the child or the empowering of the employee. The latter is more than likely an unconscious re-enactment of what happened to them when they were children. When you truly are conscious of your own genius, you will never doubt for one second the other's genius. Recall too that a child's particular passion may lie outside the restrictive realm of the school curriculum and finding a conscious hero and exceptional instructor outside the school to nurture that child's passion may be necessary; otherwise what a lost opportunity!

Model and support originality

Adam Grant (2016) in his book *Originals – How Non-Conformists Change the World* captures the nurturing of originality when he writes: "If you want your children to bring original ideas into the world, you need to let them pursue their passions, not yours." It is often the case that so-called child prodigies do not become adults who change the world because it was their parents' and teachers' passions they were following, not their own. Parents and teachers and leaders and managers do well when they exhibit pursuance of their own passions and detecting and supporting what lights up a child's learning or employee's occupational world. It is equally important that the originality of our protectors is affirmed.

Whilst persistence and practice have been advocated here, these processes certainly help children and adults to master skills but they do not learn to be original. It may be that practice makes perfect but rarely does it make new. What does appear to support originality is where children, and adults, are encouraged to develop their own beliefs and values and engage in the discovery of their own interests and passions.

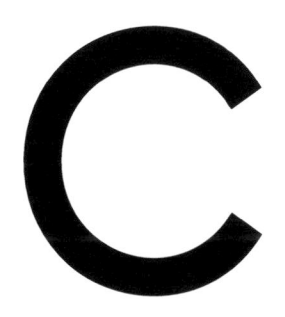

Chapter Ten:
Psychological Safety Workplace Relationships

- Fearful vs Fearless Leadership and Management
- Psychological Safety Leadership and Management

Fearful vs fearless leadership and management

As outlined, the differentiation of psychological safety from psychological safeguarding (protectivity) is fundamental to understanding the ingenious nature of each of these deep processes. Both of these processes are internal and arise in response to the nature of relationships encountered in the various holding worlds we inhabit – womb, marriage, family, school, community, workplace, church and sports and leisure clubs. When the relationships are predictably and consistently of an unconditional loving, non-judgmental, encouraging, inclusive, listening and empowering nature psychological safety will naturally arise in the child, teenager or adult. Equally, when relationships are of a hostile, conditional, critical, authoritarian or overprotective, violent and dismissive nature then psychological safeguarding of one's unique presence will automatically arise. The question that emerges is how does one move from psychological safeguarding to psychological safety?

Certainly, the person who is deeply and unconsciously safeguarding themselves from past and present threats to their wellbeing will benefit from encountering an individual who is consciously living their own life from an inner space of psychological safety. However, no expectation of the other on the part of the person who is feeling psychologically safe enough to live on their own I-land and be their own authority is crucial. Indeed, such an expectation (prescription) will wisely be seen by the other as threatening and conditional. Only the person who is psychologically safeguarded can determine when to move, initially tentatively, to experimenting to allowing psychological safety to arise and to begin to express all the unsayables and do all the undoables to this date in time. One never knows the depths of adverse experiences encountered by another, but certainly, the expression of love, belief, trust and interest in the person's life and opinions will go a long way towards paving the way for the person who has endured adverse experiences to slowly emerge from hiding.

In a book called the *Fearless Organisation* (2019) the author Amy C. Edmondson quotes interesting research and stories of fearless leaders that significantly demonstrate the power of a leader or manager who operates from an inner place of psychological safety. These leaders and managers offered an open interpersonal relationship with employees which blended care, belief, trust, respect, equality and inclusiveness, and thereby created a non-threatening relationship that presented the opportunity for each employee to begin to resurrect the psychological safety (radiant mind) they started out with when infants and children.

The road to that redemption of what is magical about human nature will be different for each member of the work organisation. Only each employee unconsciously knows of the depth and breadth of the adverse experiences they have had and the risks involved in daring to return to fearlessness. Clearly, the more individuals within an organisation that are fearless, and thereby relate to others from that psychological safety that is intrinsic to their nature, the greater possibilities there are for those in fearful or terrified places to return to fearlessness. Interpersonal truth-telling and risk-taking emerge as individuals return to their true nature of psychological safety.

I would differ from Amy Edmondson's notion that it is the work environment or the 'fearless organisation' that determines psychological safety. Organisations are systems that have no heart or head; it is individuals who have a heart and head and the relationships between members of an organisation are totally determined by the nature of each member's unconscious/conscious relationship with Self. Curiously, Amy Edmondson did not ask the question: how was it the fearless leaders she writes about came to be in such a psychological safety place? Nonetheless, Amy Edmondson's review of dozens of research studies on a wide range of work/educational/medical organisations, where there were leaders who brought their psychological safety/fearlessness to their interactions with employees/patients/students, found higher work performance, lower mortality and greater learning, and conflict being embraced as opportunity for sharing ideas and exploring differences.

Schein (2013) captured the individual nature of psychological safety when penning the lines: "Psychological safety allows people to focus on achieving shared goals rather than on self-protection." The need to keep in mind the ingenuity and creativity of both psychological safety (radiant mind expressed) and psychological safeguarding (self-protection) is paramount. The power lies within each one of us to be fearless or fearful and each of us intuitively knows, either unconsciously or consciously, which place to operate from in any interpersonal situation, be it where we live, play, learn, work, heal and pray. Psychological safety is then present when members of an organisation – whatever its nature – love, trust and believe in Self and bring that core caring relationship with Self to their relationship with others – no expectation, but certainly, curiosity. Curiosity is where a colleague who presents with challenging (psychological safeguarding) behaviours is supported to give voice to unexpressed needs, conflicts and fears and begin to dare express their own beliefs and opinions.

Psychological safety leadership and management

Throughout the book there have been particular recurring themes regarding psychological safety and the genius nature both of unconscious psychological safeguarding and conscious psychological safety solutions by individuals in homes, communities, schools, churches and workplaces. Many political, social, voluntary, health and work organisations operate from unconscious genius places, safeguarding the leaders and managers in these organisations from having to face deeper realities, but resulting in the members of these organisations suffering grave losses of love, individualisation, fairness, justice, inclusiveness, along with pressure to conform and, indeed, bullying, passivity and non-listening to unmet needs.

The foregoing list is not one of complaints but acknowledgement of the psychological safeguarding responses that are part and parcel of what happens between individuals in organisational settings. Leaders and managers of these organisations play a pivotal part in unconsciously supporting these unconscious psychological safeguarding realities and no progress is likely to happen if the leaders and managers of these organisations do not find the psychological safety to awaken to their unconscious, fear-driven responses. These awakenings have been shouting loudly for these leaders and managers to find the support and recover the psychological safety to voice and take conscious action around their own adverse childhood experiences and unmet needs before they will be in a place to bring their psychological safety into their relationships with employees and see and support them to proact on their hidden fears.

Conscious psychological safety leaders possess a vision to create workplace relationships wherein each member is loved, believed in, individualised and fully supported to fulfil their work responsibilities. When leaders and managers operate unconsciously and protectively everybody suffers to some degree and the enlightened response – which emerges when psychological safety is present – is for these governors to begin to consciously examine their own unconscious complexes and compulsions for their own and everybody else's wellbeing. But how does one start this ball rolling?

On the one hand, psychological safety is essential and, on the other hand, conscious psychological safety leaders are the key players. The *conundrum* is that psychological safety leadership primarily emerges from inner personal conscious psychological safety. When relationships within an organisation – corporate, political, religious, educational, voluntary or sports – are where leaders are operating from unconscious psychological safeguarding places, challenge may eventually come from the bottom up or from outside persons who operate from a psychological safety place. Until that happens the possibility of any real shift on either dimension is unlikely.

The development of a culture where relationships are of a nature that provide opportunities for all members of an organisation to move from psychological safeguarding to psychological safety is critical, but most especially for leaders and managers. They need the psychological safety opportunities for them to consciously examine their lives before and during their leadership years and this process is fundamental to societal wellbeing. Leaders who have unlived lives unconsciously create an environment where those in their charge dare not risk living a re-examined life.

Hopefully there are some psychological safety individuals who will non-judgmentally challenge fearful leadership and management, but the reality is that it is a high-risk venture. It may be that 'the truth will set you free' but it can also 'get you shot'. If a psychological safety society is to be created, it can only happen when there is at least a core group of conscious fearless individuals who are in an inner solid place to bring their psychological safety to others, especially those who hold power, to gradually shift from fearful to fearless leadership.

In my books *Leadership with Consciousness* and *The Mature Manager, Managing From Inside Out*, the above themes have been covered in great detail. A particular distinction was made between the roles of leaders and those of managers. Leaders are seen as visionaries while managers are practitioners – they need to make sure the job gets done; how they do that will determine whether or not it is a joy to come to work. Similarly, when leaders present their visionary projects and inventions, how much of their fearless Selves they bring to the table will largely determine the nature of and the level of commitment they elicit from their managers and other employees. When fear dominates the lives of managers and employees, they necessarily and creatively develop all sorts of psychological safeguards in the face of the threats emanating from the leaders. The vision of a leader may be realised but at what cost to the leaders themselves, the managers and the rank-and-file employees?

It is not, then, a system or an organisation that affirms or threatens the unique presence and wellbeing of its members. As explained above, a system or organisation has no heart or mind and how then can you talk with it? When a member of an organisation responds to a complaint with "It's the system, sir," my response is "How can I talk to a system? Can I be put in touch with the person who designed the system, because it is not working for me." The reality is it is individuals who run organisations and who are the sources of joy or suffering. Clearly, as outlined above, those in charge – leaders and managers – play an essential role and it is the degree of their psychological safety that will principally determine the nature of workplace relationships. This latter reality was not considered by the Nyberg Commission of Investigation into the Irish banking crisis (December 2014) which listed among the causes identified as 'group think' and a 'herd instinct'. To say that the narcissism, betrayal of trust, the greed, avarice, profit-targeted fixated mentality, the depersonalisation of both employees and customers, secretiveness and unethical behaviour can be explained by an unsubstantiated phenomenon as 'herd instinct' I find seriously worrying.

A question that is abegging of the investigators of the worst recession that Ireland has experienced is: how do they come to such a conclusion and, even more especially, how does one change 'herd instinct'? At some level – conscious or unconscious – this is a whitewash, a covering up of the true reality of what happened, that it was fear-driven individual bankers who perpetrated the disastrous response that led to the recession. The Nyberg report, carried out by individuals, failed to name any one individual even though the dogs in the street are barking their names. It is not that I want to support any witch-hunt of these individuals, but I do want to provide these persons with the non-judgment and non-threatening opportunities to reflect and critically examine the powerful emotional processes that lay at the root of their ruthless actions and, most of all, emerge from behind their walls of fear.

Outlined below are the qualities of psychological safety relationships within an organisational environment and these qualities need to become the conscious aspirations of the leaders and managers; without the latter this will not happen.

- The difference between vertical (top-down) and horizontal (person to person) communication
- The need for the promotion of employees working from the inside-out rather than the outside-in
- Active promotion of internal authority (resonance) as opposed to external authority (control)
- Separateness is the basis of psychological safety relationships within any organisation
- People before profits
- Psychological safety relationships are pathways to mutual cooperation
- Differences are the sources of creativity
- Disagreements are mirrors of unresolved childhood adverse experiences (and, necessarily, lead to conflict)
- Conflict is opportunity to find conscious solutions
- The assignment of roles rather than labels
- "There is no greater wisdom than human kindness" (Jean-Jacques Rousseau)
- Ultimately, what matters is members' wellbeing

On the crucial matter of members' wellbeing, there needs to be a conscious recognition and a lived integration of the following:

- The nature of unconscious and conscious genius
- The unique presence of each member – nothing compares!

- The creativity of fear
- The nature of psychological safety
- All human behaviour makes sense
- The power and presence of unconditional regard
- The conscious wisdom of non-judgment and active curiosity
- Genius and creativity are always present
- Each member has a unique story (inner/outer)
- The need for leadership where psychological safety is seen as paramount
- The need for management where psychological safety is seen as paramount

All of the above-listed qualities have been considered throughout the book. Certainly, the emphasis on Parents' Psychological Safety First (Chapter 5), Teachers' Psychological Safety First (Chapter 6), Psychological Safety vs Psychological Safeguarding Schools (Chapter 7) and Realising the Difference – Psychological Safety vs Psychological Safeguarding (Chapter 8) need to be reiterated for those in leadership and management roles and for the emergence of psychological safety relationships within organisations. Psychological safety and practice are the foundations for continuing personal reflection for leaders and managers who, from an inevitable emerging consciousness, will create fearless and inclusive relationships where it is a joy to come to work.

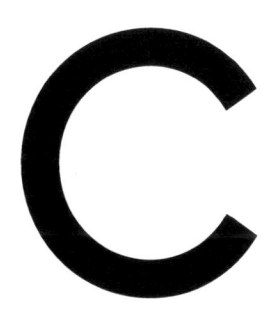

Chapter Eleven:
Beyond Psychological Safety

Beyond psychological safety

It was in a book by James Hollis that I came across his realisation: "To know that we even know what we do not know and that what we do not know frequently makes life choices for us can be a humbling and a shattering experience." His experience immediately resonated for me; indeed, it catapulted me back into a critical time in my teenage years when, standing at the gate of the family house (that was not a home) a voice from some other domain arose in me and clearly stated: "I need to go."

This 'need to go' was more than the flying of the nest that is a wise and crucial step into adulthood for young people; for me, it was a necessary escape from the distinct possibility of a lifetime entrapment of 'mending other family members' lives'. However, the emotional risks of giving expression to that wondrous thought were too great and I recall quickly repressing it and resuming my role of caring for others. Somewhat over a year later a new inexplicable conviction arose in me: become a priest. In the Catholic culture of Ireland in the 1960s having a priest in the family was the ardent wish of parents. This unexpected call provided me with what was probably the only escape route possible! Genius!

Utterly convinced, I entered an enclosed monastery. Seven years later, already ordained a deacon and a few months from being ordained a priest, I had come to a place where I had lost all belief in Catholicism. Consternation! Can I now speak the truth? I wrote a letter home expressing my reservations about certain teachings of the Catholic Church and how, given those reservations, it would be hypocritical of me to go forward to the priesthood – a little of the truth of where I truly was. My invalid mother's response was "I will die if you leave the priesthood" and my father's reaction was "I will never speak to you again." Their melancholy was terrible and my response to their letters was to go ahead with the ordination and, at a later date, volunteer to go to a house that the religious order had in South America and then to secretly disappear. Coincidentally, at this time I was coughing up blood from my lungs but medical tests could not provide any explanation for it. Was this another creation from a hidden depth?

Dreams also arise from that secret domain of knowing; indeed, I have come to see them as gifts from the soul that not only tell us where we are but also where we need to go to. The dream that propelled me into the action of finally being true to myself spoke powerfully of how much my life was in danger if I were to go ahead with the ordination. The blood symptom spoke eloquently of the life-threatening nature of 'blood (family) ties'. Silent treatment and 'being an embarrassment to the family' greeted my return home. Shortly afterwards, I literally absconded and had a difficult and extraordinary journey over the following 13 years.

Many years later, having qualified as a clinical psychologist and having therapeutically examined my own life, the above outlined experiences profoundly influenced my working with individuals who attended me and revealed their traumatic experiences. I came to marvel at the profound truth that what lies within us all – that we are always knowing, loving and wise – and what might seem to be in spite of us, shapes our lives towards, in the words of the poet Derek Walcott, meeting:

> "You will love again the stranger who was yourself,
>
> Give wine. Give bread. Give back your heart
>
> To itself, to the stranger who has loved you
>
> All your life, whom you ignored
>
> For another, who knows you by heart."

That line "who knows you by heart" is, indeed, as James Hollis says, both "humbling and shattering".

Because of the nature of our holding worlds it is often too dangerous for us to act directly out of that knowing and instead, as seen in previous chapters, we find ingenious, indirect and unconscious safeguarding ways of living. Experiences of many of the individuals I have had the privilege of accompanying in their search for conscious psychological safety holding of Self, over and over again, confirm my own experiences. Experiences such as:

- An individual terrified of change but, paradoxically, having a career in risk-management in an international financial organisation!
- Individuals who became child-care workers encountering in their care of others their own unresolved and repressed childhood traumas.

- A young man who emigrated to a country that symbolised what he so needed to consciously find for himself – 'New Zeal-and'. His father had extinguished all his natural zeal – the radiant mind of the child – with constant and harsh criticism.

- A young adult who hallucinated that he was Jesus Christ and had been in and out of psychiatric hospitals for over ten years. When I asked him what did he gain from being Jesus Christ, his spontaneous answer was "recognition". When I asked him what did he gain from being himself (say, James Murphy) his answer was "anonymity". I shook his hand and commended him for the unsung genius he is, for he had found an amazing and secretly fashioned way of being seen in a world where he had been invisible. Mysterious and magical!

- A 17-year-old teenager who had been stealing large amounts of money for over eight years, symbolically broadcasting all that had been stolen from him: the loss of both of his parents' love, the loss through sudden death of his four-year-old brother and his six-month-old sister and the loss of his primary school friends when, in spite of begging his father for several weeks to allow him to go on to secondary school with his friends, was ignored and kept back in primary school for an extra year.

I could tell story after story that support that what we do not know consciously frequently directs our life choices, and that when we find psychological safety what has been unconscious becomes conscious and open resolution of the unresolved childhood traumas now becomes possible. For me the outstanding characteristic of us as human beings is the ever present knowing and loving of ourselves that secretly manifests itself in times of threat in the most extraordinarily creative and ingenious ways.

A simple way to glimpse one's deeper and changeless nature is to ask yourself as you read the foregoing: 'Who is absorbing these words? Who is experiencing the different responses to what is written right now?' John Welwood, clinical psychologist and psychotherapist, in his book *Towards a Psychology of Awakening (2000)* provides the answer:

> "Without trying to think of an answer, if you look directly into the experiencer, the experiencing consciousness itself, what you find is a silent presence that has no shape, location or form. This nameless, formless presence – in, around, behind and between all our particular thoughts and experiences – is what the great spiritual traditions regard as our true nature, or ultimate ground, also known as the essential Self or holy spirit. This is not an experience among experiences. Instead, as a radical depth of presence and transparency, it is the ground of all experience, and it is impossible to grasp with the conceptual mind."

I believe my own struggle with my spiritual quest is similar to many other Irish people who no longer believe in Catholicism. In Ireland we do not have models for spiritual practice and yet it is essential for the continuance and the development of humanity that we bring the two sides of our nature together – absolute and relative, suprapersonal and personal, heaven and earth. While psychological work attempts to bring us out from behind our protective walls and find ourselves and provides us with glimpses of our real and core Self, spiritual practice works more directly and takes us a further step, helping us to experience a felt sense of our deeper being. In this way psychological and spiritual work are two sides of one whole quest of discovery of our spiritual nature.

Relationship mentoring or psychotherapy is the psychological path to rediscovering our true radiance and silence is the spiritual practice that helps us enter the larger sacred ground of our being that underlies all our thoughts, images, dreams and feelings. The secret is in the practice and finding time to exist on earth and to experience the heaven (soul) within us.

References

Introduction

Shenk, David. *The Genius in All of Us*. Icon Books Ltd, London, 2010

Chapter One

Welwood, John. *Towards a Psychology of Awakening*. Shambala Publications, Inc., Boston, 2000

Davies, James. *Cracked, Why Psychiatry is Doing More Harm than Good*. Icon Books, London, 2013

Leader, Darian. *Why Do People Get Ill?* Penguin Books, London, 2008

Schore, Allan N. *The Science of the Art of Psychotherapy*. Norton & Co., New York, 2013

Chapter Two

Davies, James. *Cracked, Why Psychiatry is Doing More Harm than Good*. Icon Books, London, 2013

Chapter Three

Schore, Allan N. *The Science of the Art of Psychotherapy*. Norton & Co., New York, 2012

Chapter Five

Davies, James. *Cracked, Why Psychiatry is Doing More Harm than Good*. Icon Books, London, 2013

Carlat, Daniel J., MD. *Unhinged – the Trouble with Psychiatry*. Free Press, New York, 2010

Bentall, Richard P. *Doctoring the Mind – Why psychiatric treatments fail*. Penguin, London, 2010

James, Oliver. *Not in Your Genes*. Penguin, London, 2016

Welwood, John. *Perfect Love, Imperfect Relationships*. Trumpeter, Boston & London, 2006

Chapter Six

Humphreys, Tony. *A Different Kind of Discipline*. Gill & MacMillan, Dublin, 1998

Chapter Seven

Sahlberg, Pasi. *Finnish Lesson: What the World Can Learn from Educational Change in Finland*. Teachers College Press, New York & London, 2011

Chapter Eight

James, Oliver. *Not in Your Genes*. Vermillion, London, 2016

Schore, Allan N. *The Science of the Art of Psychotherapy*. Norton & Co., New York, 2012

Gibran, Kahlil. *The Prophet*. MacMillan, New Delhi, 2015

Chapter Nine

Hollis, James. *Finding Meaning in the Second Half of Life*. Penguin, New York, 2005

Grant, Adam. *Originals – How Non-Conformists Change the World*. Penguin, Random House, New York, 2016

Chapter Ten

Edmondson, Amy C. *The Fearless Organization*. John Wiley & Sons, Inc., New Jersey, 2019

Schein, E. H. *Humble Inquiry: The Gentle Art of Asking Instead of Telling*. Berrett-Koehler Publishers Inc., San Francisco, 2013

Humphreys, Tony. *Leadership with Consciousness*. Attic Press/Cork University Press, Cork, 2011

Humphreys, Tony. *The Mature Manager, Managing From Inside Out*. New Leaf, Gill & MacMillan, Dublin, 2006

Chapter Eleven

Hollis, James. *Finding Meaning in the Second Half of Life*. Penguin, New York, 2005

Welwood, John. *Towards a Psychology of Awakening*. Shambala Publications, Inc., Boston, 2000

Books
Tony Humphreys and Helen Ruddle

Finding Sexual Realness

The Compassionate Intentions of Illness

Understanding Teenagers: Sometimes Wild, Always Wise

Relationship, Relationship, Relationship: The Heart of a Mature Society

Breakthrough: The Power of the Interrupted Relationship

Books
Tony Humphreys

Leadership with Consciousness

Self-Esteem, the Key to Your Child's Future

Leaving the Nest; What Families are all About

The Power of 'Negative' Thinking

Myself, My Partner

Work and Worth: Take Back Your Life

A Different Kind of Teacher

A Different Kind of Discipline

Whose Life are you Living?

Examining Our Times

The Mature Manager: Managing From Inside Out

All About Children: Questions Parents Ask

CDs
Tony Humphreys

Raising Your Child's Self-Esteem

Self-Esteem for Adults

Work and Self

About the Author

Dr Tony Humphreys is a Consultant Clinical Psychologist, author and national and international speaker. He began his career as a Clinical Psychologist in State Psychiatric and Psychological Services in England and Ireland and since 1990 has been working in private practice in Ireland. His practice involves working with individuals, couples, families, schools, local communities and the business community.

He is a course designer and director of two courses on communication and self-realisation and relationship mentoring in University College, Cork and Portlaoise (outreach centre) and is a regular guest lecturer in other third-level colleges, corporate organisations, wellness groups and educational systems both in Ireland and internationally, including several European countries, Turkey and South Africa. He is the author of many books on practical psychology.

Index

abandonment 48–49, 64, 72, 84–85, 86, 92
absence 22, 23
absenteeism 73, 76
abuse 48
accountability 121–122, 123
achievement 33, 67, 112, 120–121, 134, 148, 152, 154–156, 157
acting out 85, 124
addiction 11
    parents 82
    to success 114, 118, 154
    unconscious genius 19
adverse childhood experiences 52, 165, 168
affection 22
affective teaching 66, 67, 108–111
aggression 11, 30, 48–49, 50, 58, 78
    adults 40
    Screen Self and Real Self 135
    student behaviours 63
    teachers 77, 102
    tone of voice 124
    unconscious genius 19
al-one-ness 18
anorexia nervosa 37
anxiety 23, 28, 48, 86
    parents 82
    performance 105, 114, 129
    separation 30

Aristotle 112
attainment 35, 42, 46, 128–129, 134, 151
authority figures 74
autism 49
awe 28, 68, 136, 138

behavioural needs 133
being at one with Self 18
belief 18, 29, 35, 40, 148, 149, 156–157, 162, 165
belonging 107–108, 109, 132
blame 58, 102
boundaries 18, 39, 69, 70, 103
    conscious genius 10, 112
    differentiation 134
    discipline 118–119
    teachers 100, 105, 115
bridges 22, 23, 33, 58
Buber, Martin 21
bullying 53–54, 77, 97, 120, 164
burn-out 73, 76–77, 105, 121

Catholicism 172, 175
challenging behaviour 60–64, 96, 101–102, 119–120
change 134, 141–142
children
    achievement 154–156
    adverse childhood experiences 52, 165, 168
    attainment 128–129
    belief in 158
    content and context 139

    creative nature of 47–50
    difference 129–130
    early relationships 15–16
    emotional expression 109–110
    enmeshment and separateness 136–137
    fear of failure 116–117
    fearful responses 67
    future of society 97
    genius 9, 26–33
    individualisation 115–116
    inspiring 147–149
    needs 132–133
    originality 159
    psychological safeguarding 60–64
    radiance 8, 15, 68
    requests 140–141
    trauma 29, 47–48
    unique stories 67
    unloved 87–88
co-creations 146–147
co-dependence 111
cognition 134, 137–138
communication
    child's behaviour 96
    inside-out 69
    protective 56–57
    tone of voice 125, 126
    workplaces 168
compassion 11, 17, 64, 104, 106, 112

compulsions 19
conditional relating 11
conflict 17, 67, 108, 116, 128, 168
conformity 30, 33, 115, 164
connection 22, 23
conscious genius 9–12, 15, 112, 126, 158–159, 168
conscious resonance 10
consciousness 8, 18, 52–53, 59
    differentiation 133
    hero's conscious journey 23
    meaning of 66
    shift to 19, 66
    teachers 103, 105
content and context 134, 139–140
conversations 35, 38–39
courage 41
creativity 48–50, 69, 152, 163
    conflict 67
    creative needs 133
    differentiation 135
    embracing difference 128
    ever-present 169
    radiant mind 68
    repression 122
    Screen Self and Real Self 136
    workplaces 168
criticism 11, 42, 73, 116, 133
curiosity 35, 38, 44, 91, 122, 149
    active 169

differentiation 128
  homework 72
  intellectual needs 132–133
  sexual needs 132
  teachers 76
  workplaces 164
  young children 147
cynicism 105

Davies, James 27
delusions 19, 82
denial 53
dependence 22, 23, 66, 97, 133
depression 11, 15, 28, 48, 66, 86
  differentiation 134
  hero's conscious journey 23
  hero's unconscious journey 22
  male repression 109
  parents 82
  students and teachers 97
  unconscious genius 19
determination 45, 152
difference 69
differentiation 127–135
discipline 104–106, 112, 118–120
disconnection 22, 23
disorders 27, 49, 50
  see also mental illness
DSM (Diagnostic and Statistical Manual of Mental Disorders) 27

eating disorders 30, 37
economic depression 58
Edmondson, Amy C. 162, 163
education 77–80, 101–102, 111–121, 122, 146–147
    see also teachers
emergence 22, 23, 35, 97, 134, 141–142
emergence of realisations 65–70
emotion 109, 134, 137–138
emotional and social development 33, 91
emotional needs 132
emotional withdrawal 22, 30
empathy 112
empowerment 69, 161
encouragement 18, 35, 40–42, 72–73, 134, 149, 161
enmeshment 133, 136–137, 141
examination fear 143
exhaustion 73, 75–76
expectations 34, 97, 134, 140–141, 143
expression 33, 66
    differentiation 134
    emotional 57, 68, 69, 103, 109–110, 149
    hero's conscious journey 23
    hero's unconscious journey 22
    parents 89

failure 40, 134
    fear of 36, 53, 114, 116–117
    fearlessness 112, 116–118
    as opportunity 18, 31, 69, 149, 151, 158–159

radiant mind 68
　　　repression 122
　　　school cultures 121
　　　seeing attainment in 35, 42
　　　student behaviours 63
　　　young children 147
fairness 69, 164
fear 11, 66, 67, 72
　　　adults 31, 149
　　　children 15
　　　creativity of 169
　　　cynicism 105
　　　examinations 143
　　　of failure 36, 53, 114, 116–117
　　　hero's conscious journey 23
　　　hero's unconscious journey 22
　　　inducement of 120
　　　losing patience 44
　　　male repression 109
　　　ownership of 103
　　　teachers 92, 102
　　　tone of voice 124
　　　unconscious genius 19
　　　unresolved fears 28
　　　workplaces 166
fearlessness 33, 53, 57, 66, 69, 149, 164
　　　differentiation 134
　　　failure 112, 116–118
　　　heroism 45

hero's conscious journey 23
  hero's unconscious journey 22
  radiant mind 68
  repression 122
  students 97
  teachers 77, 97
  workplaces 163, 166, 169
  young children 147
feebleness 8, 15, 22, 40
Finland 123
freedom 45
Freud, Sigmund 8, 15, 28–29
frustration 73, 74, 102

genius 8, 9–11, 12, 26–33, 34
  belief in child's 35, 40
  encouraging responses to 35, 40–42
  ever-present 29, 48, 121, 151–152, 169
  individuality 20–21
  knowledge 117
  parents 34–35, 39, 148, 150–153
  recognition of own 103, 148
  unconditional love 156
  young children 147
genuineness 45, 124
Gibran, Kahlil 142
giftedness 45
Grant, Adam 159
group think 167

hallucinations 82
'hard-wired' concept 48–50
helplessness 22
herd instinct 167
heroism 35, 45, 151
hidden world 66
hiding 22, 23, 97
holding 9, 10, 44, 85, 149, 173
Hollis, James 171, 173
homework 70–73
honesty 18
hopefulness 23
hopelessness 23
hostility 57, 74, 124, 161–162
humour 69, 72–73

I-land 17, 19, 162
I-messages 120, 155–156, 157
identity 114
imagination 70
immeasurable worth 18
independence 45, 60, 66, 97, 103, 143
    differentiation 133
    hero's conscious journey 23
    hero's unconscious journey 22
    proactivity 18
    separateness 136–137
individualisation 112, 115–116, 123, 164, 165
individuality 18, 20–21, 31, 33, 40, 50, 57, 69

belonging 108
differentiation 131
overlooking 51
psychological safeguarding 68
recognition of 115
Screen Self and Real Self 136
stories 51–52
ingenuity 8, 20–21, 31–32, 34–35, 65–67, 69, 163
inner course 18, 70, 77–80
insecurity 48, 55
inside-out 11, 22, 23, 69, 134, 168
integrity 45
intellectual needs 132–133
intelligence 28, 29, 34, 50, 67
achievements 121
differentiation 133
intelligence tests 26–27, 32
knowledge 117–118
Screen Self and Real Self 136
interiority 59, 131, 146, 149, 156
teachers 78, 108, 130
tone of voice 124
introjections 15, 53
invisibility 11, 22, 23, 50
Irish banking crisis 167
irritability 15, 40, 73, 75, 77, 124, 133

James, Oliver 129
Jung, Carl 28–29, 150

kindness 69, 112, 130, 149, 168

knowledge 67, 112, 113, 117–118, 122, 133

labels 27, 30, 34, 63, 139, 168
    depression 49
    disorders 50
    mental illness 81
    students and teachers 97
    teachers 116

Lao Tzu 112

Lawrence, D. H. 157

leaders 146, 148
    achievement 155–156
    communication 57
    fearful vs fearless leadership 161–164
    passions 159
    psychological safety 149–150, 164–169
    recognition of own genius 150–153
    unconditional love 153–154

learning
    conscious psychological safety 66
    as conscious pursuit 33
    differentiation 128
    eagerness to learn 35, 44, 69, 72, 149, 154
    excitement around 35, 38
    Finland 123
    individualisation 112, 115–116, 123
    inner course 70, 77–80
    love of 35, 36, 45, 72, 91, 118, 129, 147, 148

opportunities for 35, 42–43
  repression 122
  teaching distinction 67, 121, 134, 142–144
  unconscious processes 79
liberalism 23
lived experience 18
living 22, 23
loss of control 73, 75
lovability 35, 49, 50, 68, 74, 156
love 12, 17, 28, 42, 50, 72, 143
  absence of 11
  conscious genius 112
  expression of 162
  male repression 109
  parental 88
  tone of voice 124
  workplaces 164, 165
  see also unconditional love

managers 146, 148
  achievement 155–156
  communication 57
  fearful vs fearless management 161–164
  passions 159
  psychological safety 149–150, 164–169
  recognition of own genius 150–153
  unconditional love 153–154
meditation 138
men 109

mental illness 27, 81–83, 84–85
   see also disorders
metaphors 67
Mindfulness 138
motivation, loss of 73, 76, 100, 116

neglect 48, 83, 116, 126
non-judgment 29, 69, 94, 101, 161, 169
nurture 8, 112, 149
Nyberg Commission 167

obsessions 19, 30
obsessive-compulsive behaviour 28, 88
open world 66
openness 66, 69, 124
opportunities 18, 45, 46
   failures as 69, 149, 151, 158–159
originality 149, 159
outside-in 22, 23, 134, 168
ownership 69

paranoia 19, 82, 86
parenting courses 86
parents 16, 32, 33, 48–49
   achievement 154–156
   affective and effective parenting 66
   child's educational development 144
   conscious psychological safety 34–46, 66
   creating psychological safety 149–150
   enmeshment and separateness 137

    fearful responses 67
    good enough parenting 48
    homework 70–73
    passions 159
    psychological safety first 81–90
    reaction to student behaviours 60–63
    recognition of own genius 150–153
    troubling behaviours 99
    unconditional love 153–154
    unique stories 67
    young children 147–148
passions 18, 45, 46, 131, 151, 152
passivity 11, 19, 50, 77, 93, 164
patience 18, 19, 28, 43–45, 149, 158
    differentiation 130
    homework 72–73
    parents 35
    teachers 64, 152
perfectionism 11, 15, 32, 34, 44, 50, 77
persistence 45, 68, 148, 157–158, 159
personalisation 10, 55, 84, 102, 126
physical illness 19, 30, 48, 50, 73, 76
physical needs 132
potential 157
practice 46, 148, 157–158, 159
praise 42
presence 44, 50, 130, 149, 156, 175
    hero's conscious journey 23
    hero's unconscious journey 22

    teachers 131
    unique 33, 103, 105, 114, 115–116, 136, 151, 168
priorities 131
proactivity 18, 70
projections 15, 53, 58, 99, 156
protective behaviour 12, 28–32, 50, 66, 83, 139, 149
    discipline 119
    parents 82, 90
    patience 44
    protective communication 56–57
    teachers 75, 96
psychological safeguarding 47–64, 65–68, 97
    adult beliefs 158
    children 30, 36, 60–64, 83, 85, 129–130, 139
    content and context 139–140
    differentiation 135
    enmeshment 136, 137
    genius 9–10, 11
    hero's conscious journey 23
    hero's unconscious journey 22
    hiding true Self 138, 141–142
    interiority 131
    parents 37, 40, 82, 86–89
    psychological safety distinction 161–162
    radiant mind 15–16
    repression 109, 110
    students 92
    teachers 75–76, 78, 79, 93, 98–106, 111–121, 130–131, 144
    tone of voice 124

walls 17, 153
workplaces 163–164, 166
psychological safety 8–12, 15–17
    adults 52–59
    conscious parenting 34–46
    content and context 139–140
    creating 149–150
    differentiation 127–135
    emergence of realisations 65–70
    hero's conscious journey 23
    hero's unconscious journey 22
    homework 70–73
    inner course of living 77–80
    inspiring children 148
    knowledge 113
    parents 81–90
    psychological safeguarding distinction 161–162
    relationship with Self 19
    social and emotional development 33
    teachers 73–77, 108, 111–121, 144
    tone of voice 124–126
    unresolved fears 28
    workplaces 162–169
punishment 102, 117, 118

radiance 8, 15, 40, 59, 68, 112–113, 163, 175–176
    hero's conscious journey 23
    hero's unconscious journey 22
    students and teachers 97

rationalisation 53
reading 35, 39
Real Self 133, 135–136
realisations, emergence of 65–70
rebelliousness 30, 72
receptivity 33, 50, 68, 69, 89, 110
recognition 11
relationships 15–18, 50, 51, 161–162
    education 111, 112–113
    parents 48–49
    with Self 19, 20
    separateness 136–137
    workplaces 165, 168, 169
repression 22, 52, 72, 82, 109–110, 122
requests 134, 140–141
resonance 10, 168
responsibility 19, 43–44, 58, 73, 104, 112, 123
Rilke, R. 68
risk-taking 31, 33, 69, 91, 118, 149
    hero's unconscious journey 22
    intellectual needs 132–133
    workplaces 163
    young children 147
roles 168
Rousseau, Jean-Jacques 168
Rumi 112

Sahlberg, Pasi 123
Schein, E. H. 163

school refusal 30
Schore, Alan 49
Screen Self 133, 135–136
Self 11–12, 18, 50, 58, 146
    achievements 121
    behavioural needs 133
    care of 43–44, 59, 115
    conversations with 35, 38–39
    differentiation 135
    education 79
    expression of 138
    heroism 45
    holding 173
    individuality 57
    ingenuity 21
    internal blaming 56
    learning opportunities 42–43
    parents 89, 148
    re-examination 112–113
    relationship with 19, 20, 66, 68, 112
    Screen Self and Real Self 133, 135–136
    spiritual practice 175
    student behaviours 61
    support for students 64
    teachers 73–75, 99, 100, 105, 108, 110–111, 112
    tone of voice 125
    unconditional love 11, 35, 36–38, 153
    unmet needs 141
    workplaces 164

self-esteem 50, 99, 102, 116, 118, 120
self-harm 30, 110
self-realisation 33, 58, 59
self-regard 103
separateness 18, 69, 103, 136–137, 143
    differentiation 133
    education 112, 114–115
    workplaces 168
sexual needs 132
Shaw, George Bernard 73
Shcnk, David 8
social and emotional development 33, 91
social needs 132
Socrates 31, 122
spirituality 69, 175–176
spontaneity 45, 57, 69, 149
    hero's unconscious journey 22
    radiant mind 68
    repression 122
    tone of voice 124
    young children 147
staffrooms 107–108
stories 51–54, 67, 131, 146, 169
stress 73, 75, 86, 101
success 18, 45, 69
    achievement 120–121
    addiction to 114, 118, 154
    differentiation 134
    embracing 121, 149, 158–159

repression 122
suffering 15, 83, 85
suicide 19, 53
support 64, 72–73, 112
surviving 22, 23, 97, 134
symbiotic belonging 132
symbolism 23

talents 35, 45–46, 151, 157
talking 94–95, 134
teachers 16, 33, 73–77, 89–90, 111–121
    affective and effective teaching 66, 67, 108–111
    co-creations 146–147
    conscious psychological safety 66
    creating psychological safety 149–150
    difference 130–131
    enmeshment and separateness 137
    fearful responses 67
    inner course of students 78–79
    inspirational 152
    involvement of parents 85
    need to belong 107–108
    passions 159
    psychological safety first 91–106
    reaction to student behaviours 60–63
    recognition of own genius 150–153
    relationship with Self 66
    support for students 64
    support for teachers 71, 105

teaching to the test 121–123
  tone of voice 124–126
  unconditional love 153–154
  unique stories 67
teaching/learning distinction 67, 121, 134, 142–144
teaching to the test 121–123
temper tantrums 30, 96, 130, 132
tentativeness 22
tests 118, 121–123
threats 8–9, 11, 30, 49, 52, 124, 140, 149
thriving 97, 134
tone of voice 124–126, 140–141
training 113
trauma 17, 28, 29, 47–48, 130
  hidden 85
  unresolved 31, 82, 92, 97, 173–174
trust 17, 33, 88, 156
  children 129–130
  expression of 162
  teachers 120
  workplaces 164

unconditional love 18, 29, 36–38, 69, 72, 86–87, 130
  education 112–113
  emotional needs 132
  enduring 148, 153–154
  inspiring children 148
  relationships 161
  for Self 11, 35

trust 156
unconscious genius 9–12, 19, 65–66, 75–77, 98, 154, 164, 168
unconscious resonance 10
unconsciousness 8
    differentiation 133
    hero's unconscious journey 22, 139
    learning processes 79
    meaning of 66
    shift to consciousness 19, 66
understanding 64, 70, 112, 149
    conscious genius 112
    differentiation 130, 134
    homework 72–73
unmet needs 28, 84, 132–133, 141
    emotional expression 110
    projection of 46
    students 93, 114–115
    taking responsibility for 126
    workplaces 164, 165

violence 11, 19, 30
visibility 22, 23, 33

Walcott, Derek 173
walls 9, 17, 22, 23, 29, 33, 73
wellbeing
    emotional 47, 86, 110, 143
    prioritising 66
    responsibility for 19
    students 77, 111, 115

teachers 101
　　threats to 8–9, 11, 49, 52
　　workplaces 168
Welwood, John 17, 84, 175
Wilde, Oscar 60
Winnicott, D. W. 19
withdrawal 48, 130, 132
workplaces 161–169

Printed in Great Britain
by Amazon